SUPERNATURAL™

THE OFFICIAL COMPANION
SEASON 3

SUPERNATURAL:
THE OFFICIAL COMPANION SEASON 3
ISBN 9781848561038

Published by
Titan Books
A division of
Titan Publishing Group Ltd
144 Southwark St
London, SE1 0UP

First edition February 2009
2 4 6 8 10 9 7 5 3

Supernatural ™ & © 2009 Warner Bros. Entertainment Inc.

Photo on page 142 taken by Terri Osborne.

Visit Titan Books' website:
www.titanbooks.com

Visit The CW website:
www.cwtv.com

DEDICATION
Dedicated to Owen, who at six-months-old says so much with just a look that he must have supernatural psychic powers.

ACKNOWLEDGEMENTS
Thanks are owed to many people for their contributions to this book. First and foremost, to Eric Kripke and everyone who graciously gave up their limited time to be interviewed, without whom this book would not be possible; Rebecca Dessertine, Brigitta Fry, Kaleena Kiff, Jenny Klein, Marc Klein, Jennifer Nick, and Holly Ollis for their tireless coordination; Chris Cooper, Christine Donovan, Lee Anne Elaschuk, Ivan Hayden, Robert Leader, Suzi Le Voguer, Toby Lindala, Mary Ann Liu, John Marcynuk, and Jerry Wanek for the visual materials; my family for their steadfast support; and to my editors, Jo Boylett at Titan and Chris Cerasi at DC Comics, who are a joy to work with. And special belated thanks to David Seidman for introducing me to Chris Cerasi in the first place.

Titan Books would like to thank the cast and crew of *Supernatural*, in particular Eric Kripke, Sera Gamble for the Foreword, and those who provided the wonderful visual material. And, as always, thanks to Chris Cerasi at DC Comics for all his help.

To receive advance information, news, competitions, and exclusive Titan offers online, please register as a member by clicking the "sign up" button on our website: **www.titanbooks.com** Did you enjoy this book? We love to hear from our readers. Please e-mail us at: **readerfeedback@titanemail.com** or write to Reader Feedback at the above address.

A CIP catalogue record for this title is available from the British Library.

Printed and bound in the United States of America.

SUPERNATURAL™

THE OFFICIAL COMPANION
SEASON 3

Supernatural created by Eric Kripke

NICHOLAS KNIGHT

TITAN BOOKS

CONTENTS

FOREWORD

It's fitting that our major storyline in season three was all about a contract running out. At the end of last season, our resident big bad, the Yellow-Eyed Demon, maneuvered Sam into a death match. Sam lost. Died in Dean's arms. And Dean did what Winchesters tend to do: cut a deal with a demon to bring his brother back. We started this season with a one-year clock on Dean's life. Each episode brought Dean closer to collection day and a one-way trip to Hell.

The irony wasn't lost on the writing staff. We started the season knowing that our own guild contract was about to expire. A strike looked likely. Production would shut down, possibly for the rest of the season. Maybe even for good. Yeah, we were a little distracted in the writers' room by the latest bad news from the negotiating table and by visions of going broke and having to move back in with our parents. Luckily, we could channel all that anxiety into Sam and Dean. How convenient that everything was so thematically resonant!

With that squared away, we focused on the challenge created by the nebulousness of our immediate future. We had to envision the season's story as twelve episodes, or fourteen, or the full twenty-two. Storylines were parceled out, then abbreviated. Plan Bs were hatched. When it became clear we'd be striking any day, 'Jus In Bello' was shuffled into a makeshift "Season Finale" spot, just in case.

But something else happened, too. A creatively liberated, "smoke 'em if you got 'em" attitude that you can see in the finished product. For all we knew, there was no tomorrow. If we had a burning desire to tell a certain story, better do it now. We had to ruin Christmas now. Bring back our favorite antagonists — like Gordon and Henriksen — and have fun with 'em now. Fairy tales come to life? Time loop? Episode set inside people's dreams? How 'bout one where Sam and Dean are bit players in someone else's TV show?

The guy at the head of the table, show creator Eric Kripke, was staring down an indefinite purgatory of strike lines and picket signs. He was in the mood to say, "Hell yeah, let's do it."

I'm glad we went for it. Season three ended up sixteen episodes long, interrupted mid-run by a strike that lasted over 100 days. Can't say it was the smoothest ride to the finish line. But I'm happy to report we ended up exactly where we wanted to: with Dean, screaming, on meat hooks, in Hell. I've heard that many viewers were surprised we "went there" — they thought surely we'd save Dean before that last frame. But knowing what I've just told you, can you imagine us making any other choice? Of *course* we went there.

That said, we writers (Ben Edlund, John Shiban, Cathryn Humphris, Jeremy Carver and myself, shepherded by aforementioned diabolical mastermind Eric) would never have made the attempt if we didn't have a pocket full of aces. Jensen and Jared, about whom I cannot gush enough, continually surprise us as they discover new facets of Dean and Sam. Plus, we've got exec producer Bob Singer, who can sorta do anything — direct, write, produce, play a mean air-guitar. Not to mention directors Kim Manners and Phil Sgriccia, who are so good I sometimes fear they'll be kidnapped. Serge Ladouceur, our director of photography, is consistently brilliant while working hours I can't begin to fathom. And a hardworking Vancouver crew who always deliver, who weathered a season of uncertainty and work action, and without whom all of this would look suspiciously like a blank screen.

I know I just put Eric on the list with the rest of the writers, but he gets his own paragraph, too. Not least because he gave me the job. But also because he is the creative beating heart at the center of *Supernatural* — and if that sounds slightly creepy in this context, good. His brain is beyond freaky. And his devotion to the show is total. Which, this season as every season, made all the difference.

So here you have it. Season three, from the Seven Deadly Sins to Lilith's last stand. Hope you like it. By which I mean, hope it makes you squirm, jump, grab the armrest... and feel just a little paranoid next time you have to sign a contract.

Sera Gamble
October 2008

FOCUSING SUPERNATURAL

SAM: Look, if we're going down, we're going down together.

"Season two ended with the death of the Yellow-Eyed Demon, and coming into season three the boys were now facing an onslaught by the demon populace," recalls executive producer Kim Manners, looking back to give a refresher on the impetus for season three. "What was a quest for revenge against the power that killed their mother and Sam's girlfriend now became an all out war against a demon army. We introduced Ruby and Bela. Ruby became a suspect ally, and the tale continued..."

"Season three was a really turbulent season for us — *chaotic* — for a lot of reasons, both logistically and creatively," says show creator Eric Kripke candidly of the behind the scenes atmosphere of a season that was brightened, broken, shortened, and shocking. "Speaking personally, I wrapped season two and then my wife gave birth to our son five days later. I only get two or three weeks off between seasons, and I spent those weeks as a first-time father. The sleeplessness and chaos that comes with that continued for me into the first few months of season three. I'd be lying if I said it didn't affect my ability to do the job. I think my fatigue bled its way into the early scripts."

Kripke also encountered other fatiguing demands. "I feel like we got an inordinate amount of pressure from the studio and the network," he reveals. "The studio seemed to be really focused on making sure we got picked up for season four, because with season four comes syndication. We were always on the bubble, so now the stakes were never higher. There was a lot of pressure to make sure that we kept all the Powers That Be happy. Specifically, the primary note coming from upstairs was the addition of the two female characters. I think we made a lot of missteps trying to incorporate that note, although we tried very hard to embrace it.

"For the record, we'd *always* had plans to introduce Ruby. We knew we were going to introduce a female character; we had this idea to course-correct off of where Jo was in season two. Where we felt we made a mistake was making her too innocent and too girl next door. The proper female on this show is someone who's really dangerous and a more ruthless killer than the boys. That's what Ruby was born out of, along with the notion that we've always had great success with the demons on our show. 'Let's recreate what we had with Meg in season one! Let's bring in another female demon and let her intertwine with the boys. And let's have a demon be on the good side because she becomes a real femme fatale and you don't know whether you trust her.' So she gets to have that smartass sense of humor that's fun to write and be a ruthless killer *and* still fight on the good guys' side."

DID YOU KNOW?

In a random polling of *Supernatural* cast and crew, it was determined that the most horrifying death scene of season three is in 'Time Is on My Side' when Doc Benton pries open the jogger's chest and pulls out his still-beating heart.

"I was very excited about Ruby. We'd been talking for a long time about bringing in a demon character who the boys were forced to work next to, not just exorcise and send on their way," notes producer Sera Gamble. "There's something interesting about a character that the audience can never quite get behind but also cannot deny that she's helpful. Ruby brings a lot of really good stuff to the story. I like the way she evolved in the course of the season, and I think Katie Cassidy did a really good job with her."

Manners wholeheartedly agrees. "I thought she brought a lot of danger to the character, a lot of sass. She had a strength and a charm that I loved. And I thought there was a great heat between Ruby and Sam. There was some sexual tension there that was never really [stressed], it just kind of happened."

"Ruby was always part of the plan," Kripke reiterates, "but then the note came from upstairs, 'Find another female.' And we said, 'But we have a female and she threads into the mythology!' And the note was, 'No, two women, not just one. Two boys, two girls.' I'm not entirely sure what the logic was, but I think maybe it was, 'Well, maybe one of the girls won't work out, so you'll have a backup.'"

As it happened, at that time co-executive producer Ben Edlund was breaking his episode, 'Bad Day at Black Rock'. "We knew we had this character Bela, who was going to be, for all intents and purposes, a supernatural cat burglar. We really liked the character," professes Kripke, "and we really were taken with the notion of a player in the *Supernatural* world who isn't a hunter, but who is much more

Above

Ruby (Katie Cassidy) wields a blade that's just as deadly to demons as the Colt's bullets.

Above

Bela (Lauren Cohan) is perturbed that Dean tricked her into touching the cursed rabbit's foot.

interested in the value of the objects than the monsters themselves. We thought that was an intriguing character that we hadn't seen before. She was intended as a one off, but we thought there was enough interesting real estate there, so we said, 'Well, let's make her the other lead female. She's right there in front of us and we think she has potential.'

"When Lauren Cohan came in to audition, hers was one of those auditions that you were just excited about. You drove home thinking, 'I can't believe we found this girl — she's lightning in a bottle!' She was an actress of such depth and skill. We showed her to the studio and network and they flipped over her. It felt like such a slam-dunk. But I think we did a great disservice to the character because we didn't spend enough time thinking about how to tie her into the boys' story. It's a road show and we're in a different town every week, so if you're going to run into the same character over and over again, you better have a damn good reason. And it better be the *same* reason, because if it's a different reason every time then it starts to feel like, 'Hey Bela, I can't believe we keep running into you!' We started to get crushed under the weight of the absurdity of it. When Ruby shows up, you don't need to explain it because she's tied in with the demon mythology. When Bobby shows up, it's because the boys called him for help. But with Bela you needed to explain it every time, and it started to get more and more difficult to write our way around that.

"The other mistake we made was we had so much fun with an antagonistic female and were so taken with a woman who could screw the boys over at every turn that we weren't careful about balancing it and made her screw over the boys so badly — put them in life-threatening danger over and over again and let her get the upper hand on them over and over again — that she became unlikable to the fans because she was irredeemable."

Right from the end of her first episode, Bela shooting Sam without any hesitation or remorse set her up as an instant she-needs-to-die enemy, yet then she came back to take the boys to a high society gala… "We thought we were being clever," Kripke admits. "For that little moment where Dean says, 'You're not going to shoot anyone,' and then she does, we thought, 'Wow, that's surprising, that shows someone who's badass!' We didn't really think through the implications as carefully as we should have. For a character that's going to come back and slow dance with Dean, that's not the best notion. You couldn't come back and have a funny effervescent episode where they all work together because she just tried to have them killed two times. People watch the show for Sam and Dean, so a character who makes them feel like idiots is not a character that people are going to warm up to.

"Had we figured it out in time, I think we could have made Bela work," Kripke believes. "You create all these things with enthusiasm and the best of intentions, but hindsight is twenty-twenty. I'd work with Lauren again in a heartbeat. She worked so valiantly under all of the obstacles we placed on her.

"We were also in a turbulent place creatively because we'd just killed our main bad guy," adds Kripke. "We were in this odd place in the first half of the season when there really was no main bad guy. There really was no mythology to speak of outside of 'the demons are in chaos because they don't have a leader'. We had this notion to make it reflect real-world terrorism cells; that was the idea. They were not necessarily organized, and there was a danger in that, that they could be everywhere. Each one has a different motive. There's a lot of dialogue in the first five or six episodes that talks about this chaotic new landscape of demonkind. The notion is, 'How do you fight a war without a front?' But it didn't quite work for a couple of reasons.

"For one thing, I should just write what I know. I don't know much about the politics of real-world terrorism. I'm not a ripped-from-today's-headlines kind of writer. I like

HELL OF A DEAL

"It gave us a lot of effective emotional context to play with throughout the season," says Eric Kripke of the effect Dean's deal with the Crossroads Demon had on the brothers. "Sam had to grow up and support his older brother for a change. It was stressful for him, realizing that he wasn't going to have Dean forever. It forced him to be more independent. Dean was really immature about eating cheeseburgers and banging girls, then he admitted he was terrified but didn't feel he was worth saving, and finally he realized he *was* worth saving. He had to learn throughout the season that he's worth something in his own right, not just as John's son and Sam's protector, but as his own person who deserves his own life. It probably would have been a healthy thing for him, but unfortunately he went to Hell, and that's going to set him off in a whole new dark direction…"

Above

Dean (Jensen Ackles) can't help but wonder if Ben is his son.

old stories and old legends, that's where my strengths are, so I believe that lack of authenticity made its way to the screen.

"The second thing was because of one of the other notes that came from upstairs, which was, 'Make the show bigger. Increase the scope of the show. It feels too insulated with just these two guys and these creepy little rooms, and we're suffocating. Let's open up the show with more characters, bigger scope,'" explains Kripke. "They pointed to our Hollywood episode and our two-part season finale, 'All Hell Breaks Loose'. 'Look at all that scope! We want that epic kind of scope.' So we said, 'That's really going to cost you a lot of money,' and they said, 'You gotta go for the scope. If a few episodes go over budget then so be it.' That's where that whole notion of wartime came from. All these demons are loose from the Devil's Gate, let's ratchet that up.

"I wrote the season opener, 'The Magnificent Seven', with that wartime scope note in the front of my mind, and that's why you have Isaac and Tamara. We just thought we'd start trying out people, so we tried out this hunter couple and we thought maybe Tamara would come back, and we'd have seven demons because seven is better than one. We just started throwing scope at the problem. We went *so* over budget with that first episode, but it's our fault; we should've pulled the fire alarm and stopped pre-production and rewrote the script. The studio very rightfully flipped out. They said, 'Whoa, when we said over budget, we didn't say *this*.' So they immediately clamped down and said, 'You *cannot* go over budget for the rest of the season, you *have* to keep things on the number.' But that throws a grenade creatively, because how do you do the scope and the size that you were supposed to do when you don't have the money to do it? So we'd set up this whole war that we realized by the second episode we couldn't even come close to paying off.

"There are some really good episodes in the first third of the season, but there are some that I don't love, and it's not my favorite start of a season," Kripke confesses. "I would certainly put 'Red Sky at Morning' on my list of worst *Supernatural* episodes.

I don't think we had a Hall of Shame episode in season two, so it was sort of discouraging to have a Hall of Shame episode in season three."

Executive producer Bob Singer didn't find it nearly as discouraging. "We had just that one episode that was not quite up to snuff. That's a pretty good record, and I'm really happy about that."

Kripke reconsiders. "I thought 'The Kids Are Alright' was a very good episode, 'Bedtime Stories' was really good, and 'Bad Day at Black Rock' was very funny. But there was something [about those first six episodes] that I can't quite put my finger on... Maybe because the overall mythology was kind of in this weird no man's land, or maybe because we had to make such huge compromises on every script to wrestle it down to budget. People probably watch them and enjoy them and don't see the pain that I felt during those episodes."

"You're constantly moving forward and you just learn your lessons and you try to do better the next time. We hit our stride midway through," Gamble believes.

"If you look at episodes seven through sixteen, those are really good episodes," Kripke emphasizes. "It's something I can stand behind proudly and say, 'That's *Supernatural*.' We gave up this idea of trying to present the huge scope of war and started focusing on stories that we knew we could tell well — these very down and dirty, lean and mean stories. If we were going to tell war stories, we were going to figure out creative ways to shoot them, like 'Jus in Bello', where there is a huge war, but it's all outside the building and you're trapped inside. Rather than trying to service this terrorism metaphor that wasn't working, we started immediately

DID YOU KNOW?

In a random polling of *Supernatural* cast and crew, the changeling children in 'The Kids Are Alright' were voted the scariest monsters of season three.

Above

The Crossroads Demon (Sandra McCoy) informs Sam that she doesn't actually hold the contract on Dean's soul.

producing a new big bad. So Lilith started being mentioned, at first not even as 'Lilith'. We always knew we were going to bring in a new head demon by the end of the season, and I don't know if we even necessarily brought her in sooner than we thought we would, but it was just so refreshing to get back on firm ground where you knew there was a bad guy and you knew there was a plan.

"When you look at the second half of the season, that's when I think the really creative storytelling starts happening. 'Dream a Little Dream of Me', 'Jus in Bello', 'Mystery Spot', 'Ghostfacers'... They start becoming these really fun stories again." As they were writing those stories, the impending writers' strike became a reality, which could've been a disaster. "Fortunately, I feel we found our footing just in time to get hit by the strike," he reflects. "The strike was very bad, but also good. To lay everybody off right before Christmas was a real dark moment for us. But on the personal side, I got to spend that time with my son and get to know him, just being a dad... and I'm very thankful for that.

"I think the strike was actually creatively useful, because it let us focus on the storyline we needed to pay off, which was Dean's deal. So we were able to have dad call from the dead, and really start hitting the beats of where Dean and Sam's heads were closing in on Dean's deal. Once you had that one clear thing to concentrate on, it made a lot of the creative decisions easy. We could focus on one thing, do it well and tell a good story right. I feel we came back from the strike with a lot of momentum, telling really good stories that propelled us into the finale.

"But all of that's still outweighed by the guilt we feel that we put our crew out of work," Kripke adds. "That just really, really sucked. But we got our crew back and everyone seems to be okay."

"Coming back after the strike was a little bit weird," Gamble observes. "I was afraid that it was going to be really chaotic, but Bob and Eric run a really tight ship, and it was all hands on deck. Everyone was very focused, very calm." Singer credits the strike for refreshing the actors too. "They were ready to go, and we hit the ground running with the scripts," he says. "I think everyone was just really happy to be back."

Jared Padalecki supports Singer's assertion. "Big picture, the strike was bad, but

Above
There's a demon war brewing outside, and Agent Henriksen (Charles Malik Whitfield) is trapped in the middle of it.

LIGHTING THE DARKNESS

"For season three, the network wanted a more colorful look," explains Serge Ladouceur, director of photography. "We'd already pulled away from the strong gothic look of the beginning of season one, and in season two we established a look that I think suited the show. But the network wanted it brighter, and I went along with it and made it work. The dark scenes were still shot dark, so we were cautious in keeping the direction of our show."

"None of us really cared for going brighter," comments Phil Sgriccia. Kim Manners concurs. "It may have pleased the network, but it didn't please us."

Jensen Ackles, however, is sure that *Supernatural*'s look will always be great with Ladouceur lighting the show. "He's a genius. We're lucky to still have him. For him to constantly evolve his lighting with the show and change it accordingly, that's a testament to his talent."

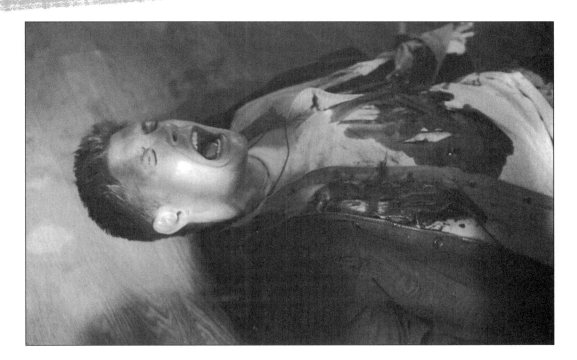

for me personally, it was a much-needed vacation. Even when I'm not shooting the show, I'm auditioning for movies or meeting with this producer or that director or this writer. Since before I turned eighteen, I've been caught up in this crazy business that is Hollywood, so it was a nice break."

"As I look back on the strike," says Kripke, "with the season finale sort of evolving from the real-life concerns of the strike and budget, I truly feel that episode benefited as a result. For a long time, when we thought we were going to have twenty-two episodes to tell the story, Sam was going to save Dean from Hell, maybe even before the season finale, but at the cost of activating his demonic powers. And they had to take on Lilith, but Sam was not thinking, 'Should I use my powers or should I not?' He was fully activated, and Dean had to worry that it was really dangerous, like playing with this nuclear bomb. That was the original conception. Then when they went up against Lilith, maybe they would've survived and maybe they wouldn't have.

"Because of the strike, we knew we weren't going to be able to develop Sam's story far enough to make him credibly want to suddenly turn on his powers. His walk down the dark side has to be this really slow, considered walk, and we didn't want to rush that because there's a lot of story to be had out of that. So somewhere around episode seven or eight, when it really looked like the strike was going to happen and we wouldn't have the time to save Dean, we knew we needed an alternative, so we said, 'What if he *doesn't* save Dean?' That was when it first came up. So we decided to leave Dean in Hell, let him take sort of a breather in Hell."

Tune in to season four to find out just how long Dean's "breather" lasts... or if he's even breathing *at all* anymore. ✍

Above

Lilith's hellhounds rip out Dean's soul.

Opposite

Sam and Dean *not* experiencing déjà vu in 'Mystery Spot'.

DID YOU KNOW?

In a random polling of *Supernatural* cast and crew, the favorite episode question resulted in a four-way tie between 'Bad Day at Black Rock', 'A Very Supernatural Christmas', 'Mystery Spot', and 'Ghostfacers'.

THE EPISODES

RUBY: Does anyone have a breath mint? Some guts splattered in my mouth while I was killing my way in here.

SEASON 3 REGULAR CAST:

Main
Jared Padalecki (Sam Winchester)
Jensen Ackles (Dean Winchester)

Recurring
Katie Cassidy (Ruby)
Lauren Cohan (Bela Talbot)
Jim Beaver (Bobby Singer)
Sterling K. Brown (Gordon Walker)
Michael Massee (Kubrick)

THE MAGNIFICENT SEVEN

Written by:
Eric Kripke

Directed by:
Kim Manners

Guest Cast: Gardiner Millar (Bouncer/Wrath), Tiara Sorensen (Waitress/Greed), Allison Warnyca (Random Shopper), Monique Ganderton (Redhead), Ben Cotton (Businessman/Pride), C. Ernst Harth (Heavy Set Man/Sloth), Katya Virshilas (Hot Girl/Lust), Michael Rogers (Bartender/Gluttony), Peter Macon (Isaac), Josh Daugherty (Walter Rosen/Envy), Caroline Chikezie (Tamara)

It's been five days since hundreds of demons escaped from Hell... and Sam and Dean are getting antsy wondering *when* the war will begin. But with only one year left to live, Dean has other things on his mind, such as casual sex and cheeseburgers. Sam is busy trying to get Dean out of his deal with the Crossroads Demon, but he's interrupted by Bobby, who's got a lead on some demon activity in Nebraska.

The hunters meet up at a farmhouse, where they find a family watching TV, all starved to death... as if they'd been too lazy to get up to eat. They meet up with a hunter couple, Isaac and Tamara, but they don't exactly hit it off since the hunters blame the Winchester brothers for "letting" the Devil's Gate get opened. Things get weirder when an otherwise sane woman beats another woman to death over a pair of green shoes. Meanwhile, a mysterious blonde woman is stalking Sam.

Bobby and the boys track the demon responsible for the shoe murder to a bar. Isaac and Tamara show up and go inside, where they're caught in a bar full of demons. The demons force Isaac to kill himself by drinking drain cleaner. Bobby smashes his car through the bar's wall and he and Sam rescue Tamara while Dean captures a demon.

Back at Tamara's house, they interrogate the demon and discover they're up against demonic manifestations of the Seven Deadly Sins. After they exorcise Envy, the other demons attack, but the four hunters hold their own, and then the mysterious blonde shows up to save Sam, brandishing a demon-killing knife.

After all the demons have been exorcised, Sam suggests they go see a hoodoo priestess to get Dean out of his deal, but Dean tells him if they break the deal, Sam dies. Sam is pissed that Dean gave up his life for him, but Dean's happy Sam's alive, so he suggests they make the best of his last year and go raise a little hell...

DEAN: Truth is, I'm tired, Sam. And, I don't know, it's like... there's a light at the end of the tunnel.
SAM: It's Hellfire, Dean.
DEAN: Whatever. You're alive... and I feel good. For the first time in a long time. I got a year to live, Sam. I'd like to make the most of it. So what do you say we kill some evil sons of bitches and we raise a little hell, huh?

DID YOU KNOW?

'The Magnificent Seven' features the most demons of any *Supernatural* episode, even more than in 'Jus in Bello' and 'All Hell Breaks Loose, Part Two'. Visual effects supervisor Ivan Hayden reports that the demon clouds in the teaser were made up of "hundreds of individual demons".

"I thought using the Seven Deadly Sins was a great idea," exclaims composer Chris Lennertz. "It was a great way to start the season. That episode was fun for me because we gave a slightly different sound to all the different sins, like Sloth was a slow, lumbering, creepy low-end thing. And when we first introduced Ruby, I wanted to give her something a little otherworldly, so I used a scraping metal sound, which was really a quarter scraped across a cymbal."

Although her demon aspect gave her an otherworldly quality, Ruby had more of a hunter persona. "She was like a female version of the boys," asserts costume designer Diane Widas. "Sexy, but down to earth. We tried to keep her in dark tones so she could hide in the shadows and things like that. Usually she was in pleather jackets and narrow jeans so she could be really active, since she kicks ass."

"Katie Cassidy is just beautiful," states key makeup artist Shannon Coppin. "We try to make the hunters not really look made up, but she has the longest eyelashes I've ever seen, so even with no makeup she looks like she's got makeup on. But she was allowed to be prettier because she's supposed to blend in with the people on the street. Ruby just picked a hot body to possess."

"Katie, God bless her, wasn't the most physically coordinated girl I'd ever met," notes executive producer Kim Manners. "So Lou Bollo, our stunt coordinator, trained her hard to do that fight scene with the knife... and she did a wonderful job." Bollo agrees. "We showed her some knife moves and she went from this really nice-looking, quiet person into this aggressive lethal weapon. It was fun taking her through that."

Above

Dean locks and loads.

MUSIC

'Hells Bells' by AC/DC

'You Ain't Seen Nothing Yet' by Bachman-Turner Overdrive

'Mean Little Town' by Howling Diablos

'I Shall Not Be Moved' by J.B. Burnett

When Ruby makes her deadly entrance, it's instantly obvious that she's not wielding just any knife. "The knife kills demons completely — it's a hand-to-hand version of the Colt," explains creator Eric Kripke.

"I bought elk antlers," notes prop master Chris Cooper, "because we wanted to do something decent sized for the knife handle. The blade was engraved on both sides, but basically it's just gibberish."

Cassidy was fortunate she didn't reveal her demon side in 'The Magnificent Seven', otherwise she would've had to try out her new fighting skills while wearing black contact lenses. "It took a long time for me to get used to them," admits Peter Macon. "You could still see through them because they had a hole in the middle, but it was really freaky walking around with those other demons at the lunch tent. It was even hard to look at myself in the mirror with those on. But it was a lot of fun."

Macon had even more fun with the drain cleaner scene. "When the demons made me drink that drain cleaner — which was just Gatorade and Jell-o — some people on the set were gagging. And we had to do it twice. At first they were cheering, but then they were like, 'That's so disgusting!' It was really fun chugging the 'drain cleaner' and freaking everybody out. That was probably the most memorable part of the episode."

Bobby driving his car through the bar wall was also quite memorable. "There was a funny incident with that," shares Bollo. "We had him smash in there and

everything had gone well, then we came to the point where Jim Beaver had to jump in and drive the car out because we had to see his face. So they're rolling for it and he was so energized that he left Jensen behind. As the car pulls out, Dean's left stranded at the bar with all the demons! It was very funny."

DEAN: I'm just gonna ask it again... Who was that masked chick? Actually, the more troubling question would be, "How come a girl can fight better than you?"
SAM: *Three* demons, Dean. At once.
DEAN: Hey, whatever it takes to get you through the night, pal.

"We're constantly aware that none of this is real," observes Jim Beaver. "Before we do a heavy dramatic scene, someone's coming up and combing your hair and making sure your buttons are buttoned, and somebody's coming up and applying fake blood... so it's impossible to get caught up in the story the way someone who is watching the show does. A lot of the magic is reserved for the fans.

"I was watching 'The Magnificent Seven' on TV, and some innocent victim was being taken over by a demon, with the whole black smoke going into his mouth thing. And I thought, 'When they shot that, it was just a guy lying on the ground, writhing around with his mouth open.' But then you add the music, the lighting, and that really cool visual effect, and I'm like, 'Whoa, look at that!' When we're doing it, it's a little goofy. But then you watch it and you go, 'Man, that looks like it really happened.' That's pretty impressive." ✦

THE KIDS ARE ALRIGHT

Written by:
Sera Gamble

Directed by:
Phil Sgriccia

Guest Cast: Margot Berner (Katie Keel), Nicholas Elia (Ben Braeden), Cindy Sampson (Lisa Braeden), Alberto Ghisi (Ryan Humphrey), Kathleen Munroe (Dana Keel), Megan Bowes (Changeling #1), Desiree Zurowski (Annette), Todd Thomson (Richard), Daniel Brodsky (Changeling #3), Michelle Grigor (Changeling #4/Dakota Ridgeway), Mitchell Duffield (Changeling #2), Susie Wickstead (Mom #1), Stacy Fair (Mrs. Ridgeway)

Dean drags Sam to Cicero, Indiana, so he can visit Lisa Braeden, a memorable girl he hooked up with close to nine years ago. However, Dean is stunned when he meets Lisa's eight-year-old son, Ben, who bears a striking resemblance to him, both in physical appearance and personality. Then the mysterious blonde — Ruby — reappears and tells Sam there's also a job in Cicero.

Sam and Dean investigate and discover that a changeling is snatching kids from their homes and replacing them with her own changeling children. The young creatures assume the appearance of the children they replace, and then use their sucker mouths to feed on the sleeping mothers, slowly draining their synovial fluid.

Dean bonds with Ben, but soon after the boy is replaced with a changeling. The Winchester brothers track the changeling mother down to an abandoned house, where they find all the abducted children in the basement, locked in cages. They free the children, and then Ben helps the others escape while Dean and Sam fight the changeling. They use a flamethrower to light her on fire, and all her offspring burn up along with her.

Lisa assures Dean that Ben is not his child, but asks if he'll stick around. Dean is sorely tempted, but that's not the life for him, especially since his life is almost over. Meanwhile, Ruby helps Sam learn that everyone his mother ever knew is dead, then she shocks him by revealing herself to be a demon... and claims she can help him save Dean's life.

SAM: So let me get this straight. You want to drive all the way to Cicero just to hook up with some random chick?
DEAN: She's a yoga teacher. It was the bendiest weekend of my life!

"'The Kids Are Alright' was flat-out creepy scary," declares editor Tom McQuade. "Masterful horror, masterful suspense!"

"For the children in 'The Kids Are Alright', once you saw them in their true form, with those big eyes and that lamprey-like sucker mouth, that was just so disturbing," states creator Eric Kripke. "I give [visual effects supervisor] Ivan Hayden a lot of credit, because originally I was saying, 'Just have their faces get pale and have dark circles under their eyes.' And Ivan said, 'I think we should really go further.' Normally I say less is more, and restrain our various departments from going too far because I

DID YOU KNOW?

Jensen Ackles doesn't scare easily, but a scene from 'The Kids Are Alright' made him squeamish. "The scene that stands out is when the guy gets thrown back against the table saw and you see it start ripping his shirt open, and you hear the crunching noises as it rips through the ribcage..."

Above
Dean does the math
to see if Ben could be
his son.

don't want it to be over the top, but Ivan was a real dog with a bone on that one. He said, 'No, no, no, you're not picturing what I'm picturing, this is really going to be cool. Let me go for it,' and talked me into it. I saw the first test of it and called him immediately and said, 'You're right, I'm wrong. Thank God you did this. Thank God I didn't stop you, because this is one of the cooler monsters we've ever done.'"

Fortunately for co-executive producer Phil Sgriccia, the real-life kids were much less creepy than their onscreen reflections. "I always have fun with the kids," Sgriccia says. "Sometimes I bring a little fart machine and put it under somebody's chair. I goof around with them to take the edge off the work."

"It was really amazing to see Nicholas Elia — the little boy that played Dean's 'son' — together with Jensen, because some of his mannerisms were dead on. The casting was really good," states sound editor Donald Painchaud. "The whole thing was for him to look like Little Dean," says costume designer Diane Widas. "It was funny, because I was going to make him a little canvas three-quarter jacket like Dean wears, but then I went out and I found the jacket [he wound up wearing]. And he did look like Little Dean once we put it all together."

Sgriccia would like to see Elia come back. "I really enjoyed working with Nicholas and Cindy Sampson. I think Ben's gotta be Dean's son, because when you get good characters with good actors playing the role and then they don't die, it's always nice to think they could come back."

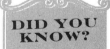

DID YOU KNOW?

When Sam is researching his mother's friends, he asks about a Robert Campbell and learns that the man died on July 19th, which is Jared Padalecki's birthday.

Above

Dean's a little disconcerted on meeting Ben.

Sera Gamble comments, "People always ask me if Ben is actually Dean's kid. I think people really want him to be. I guess the door's always open that Lisa could've been lying…"

DEAN: It's a cool party.
BEN: Dude, it's so freakin' sweet. And this moon-bounce — it's epic.
DEAN: Yeah, it's pretty awesome.
BEN: You know who else thinks they're awesome? Chicks. It's like hot-chick city out there.

It certainly seemed like Lisa had a strong motive for wanting Dean to stick around with that kiss she laid on him. "That wasn't in the script," Sgriccia shares. "We added the kiss, and we didn't tell Jensen it was going to happen. The mischievous side of me wanted to see what Jensen would do. I always say, 'You turn on the camera and you get a little magic.' And what you see on the film is his first take when she kisses him.

"We held the kiss off until we came to his side. Then she runs up and plants him one on the lips. I talked to Cindy beforehand and said, 'I think you need to kiss him here,' and she goes, 'What?' And I said, 'Yeah, I think you need to kiss him. Not a slutty kiss, just a nice, tender kiss to say thanks for saving my son.' She was aghast

MUSIC

'40,000 Miles' by Goodnight City
'If It Ain't Easy' (instrumental) by Steve Carlson

at first and flustered a little bit, and I said, 'What, you don't want to?' And she said, 'Of course I want to kiss him!'"

"I haven't had to do a lot of rewrites on *Supernatural*," asserts composer Jay Gruska, "but that there was a rewrite at the end of the show where there's an emotional moment between the two of them. The first time through didn't quite work because it had a little too much in an emotional sense. So I had to touch up the cue, pull back a couple of notches, which is always something you have to be careful about on the show, because it's gotta pull at the heartstrings without hitting you over the head with a sledgehammer." ✐

BEING HUMAN IS DELICIOUS

"Ruby was really fun to write," notes producer Sera Gamble. "I had the sense that she was a demon who was really stoked to be back topside. So all the things about being in a human body were really cool to her... Like eating French fries was delicious, driving really fast in cars would feel delicious, and you just knew she was going to go trying on lots of delicious clothes. She was somebody who was very much enjoying everything about being in a human body.

"She was a very scary kickass fighter, also. I think that on our show female characters tend to last longer if they're presented as antagonists."

BAD DAY AT BLACK ROCK

Written by:
Ben Edlund

Directed by:
Robert Singer

Guest Cast: John F. Parker (Elderly Man), Forbes Angus (Manager), Stephen Dimopoulos (Foster), Christian Tessier (Wayne), Hrothgar Mathews (Grossman), Jon Van Ness (Creedy)

A hunter named Kubrick visits Gordon Walker in prison, and Gordon convinces him that "Sam Winchester must die…" Sam tells Dean about his encounter with Ruby, who is angry that Sam didn't kill the demon, but Sam insists she could be useful. A call comes in on their dad's cell phone and they learn that John's storage room near Buffalo, New York, has been broken into. They track down the robbers and discover that the stolen item is a cursed rabbit's foot, which provides extremely good luck until lost, but once lost the previous owner dies within a week.

Unfortunately, Sam handles the foot before they find out it's cursed. Dean takes advantage of Sam's luck by having him scratch lottery tickets, which all win, but then a female thief steals the foot… Sam's luck turns bad and he has a series of mishaps, from scraping his knees to setting himself on fire! Dean has to get the rabbit's foot back — and destroy it — before Sam gets himself killed. With Bobby's help, he figures out that the thief is a woman named Bela Talbot. Dean breaks into Bela's apartment and grabs the rabbit's foot. It gives him incredible luck, so even though Bela shoots at him, he escapes unharmed.

Meanwhile, Kubrick has taken Sam prisoner. Just as Kubrick prepares to shoot him in the head, Dean arrives and (luckily) saves the day. They prepare to destroy the rabbit's foot, but Bela arrives and demands Dean hand it over. She shoots Sam in the shoulder to show how serious she is. Dean tosses the rabbit's foot at her and Bela instinctively catches it, cursing herself. She has no choice but to let the brothers burn the cursed object, though she also steals their winning lottery tickets.

Kubrick visits Gordon again and they plot Gordon's escape…

DEAN: So you know the truth about what's really going on out there, and this is what you decide to do with it? You become a thief?
BELA: I procure unique items for a select clientele.
DEAN: Yeah. A thief.
BELA: No… A great thief.

"We had such a great time doing 'Bad Day at Black Rock'," enthuses executive producer Robert Singer. "That was my favorite of the year. Over the course of my career I've done heavier stuff, so to be able to do something that had a lighter touch to it was a real kick for me, especially the big fight where the boys are fighting over the rabbit's foot with the two heavies. That was really difficult to shoot, but I'd do a

Opposite

Dean can hardly believe such a little thing caused so much trouble.

DID YOU KNOW?

Lauren Cohan doesn't have a lucky rabbit's foot, but she has a lucky stuffed animal that she's had since she was born. "When I don't know where that is, like if I've moved and things are still disorganized, I feel unsettled," she shares. "If I know its whereabouts, I feel much safer."

shot, then I'd giggle to myself.

"I loved [co-executive producer] Ben Edlund's script," Singer says. "Ben is a genius at writing oddball, fun stuff like that," agrees script coordinator Michael Moore. "Ben's a great guy," adds consulting producer Laurence Andries, "and he has such a specifically twisted way of looking at the world that's both ironic and funny without being mean-spirited."

"I'm the funny episode guy, as a rule," admits Edlund. "Basically I wanted this to be a screwball comedy." Creator Eric Kripke was "enamored with that idea. This is the first time we'd ever done anything like this, where Ben said, 'I want to tell an episode of *Supernatural* where there's no monster whatsoever, where it's just about this lucky rabbit's foot that gets really lucky and then gets really unlucky.'" Edlund thinks the episode "came out great. The concept is funny, but the direction and delivery was a huge part of it working. Jensen's affinity for comedy is really remarkable, I think. And Jared did a really wonderful job. I wasn't sure if the shoe gag wasn't too quiet a gag to live in the show. It felt a little different, which I think is why people remember it."

"It was hard not to laugh during that scene," recalls Jared Padalecki. "That was a fun episode to film, and I got to explore the humorous side of Sam. But I've never been comfortable doing humor — I consider myself a dramatic actor — but Bob

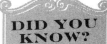

DID YOU KNOW?

This episode features Dean's memorable one-liner, "I'm Batman!" Ackles, who notes he wore Batman pajamas as a little kid, shares another one-liner. "We had one take where Sam says, 'You're Batman,' and I'm like, 'And you're my Robin,' but they didn't put that in..."

Above

Bela insists Dean returns the rabbit's foot.

Singer directed it, so I knew I was in capable hands. I just trust the director and the writers and go with it." Jensen Ackles thinks "it was Jared's funniest episode, which I like because Sam doesn't really get to be funny very often. It was a bit goofy at times for *Supernatural*, but I really enjoyed it as an audience member. I can watch 'Bad Day at Black Rock' over and over again!"

"I think 'Bad Day at Black Rock' was one of the funniest episodes we've ever done," proclaims producer Sera Gamble. "I loved the scene where Sam can't even scratch his nose, and I loved the way Ben introduced Bela." Singer is also fond of Bela's introduction. "I personally loved that character, and I loved working with Lauren Cohan."

> BELA: Thanks very much. I'm out one and a half million, and on the bad side of a very powerful, fairly psychotic buyer.
> DEAN: Wow... I really don't feel bad about that. Sam?
> SAM: Nope. Not even a little.

Singer loved working with Michael Massee, too. "He was great because he totally brought his own reality to it. This episode and that villain were quite out there, but he so believed in the character that he imbued Kubrick with this total honesty, so it absolutely worked." Massee elaborates, "When you work on something that can be complete fantasy, the challenge is to make it human and make it real, and then the supernatural things can come alive in a way that's not too out there."

Even John Winchester's storage room had elements that were a little out there,

MUSIC

'Vaya Con Dios' by Mary Ford & Les Paul

'Women's Wear' by Daniel May

such as the inclusion of the monkey prop from Harvelle's Roadhouse. Production designer John Marcynuk reveals that "the monkey was somewhere in the back, as if somehow dad might still be alive and found it in the remnants of the bar. There are some little jokes in there. One little touch I brought into that episode was every time good luck happens, there's a rabbit in the scene. The Vietnam vet has a patch with a rabbit on it and the lottery cards have magician's hats with rabbits coming out of them. There are other places in the episode that if you look, you can find them."

Kripke feels the storage room is "a really interesting treasure trove of potential weapons and things. I'm actually surprised we haven't gone back there." Maybe that's a hint of things to come... ⚿

THE LUCK OF JARED

Jared Padalecki doesn't carry a lucky rabbit's foot, but he probably would if someone had told him during his formative years that they're truly lucky...

"Whenever I drive under a yellow light and whenever I'm getting on a plane, I kiss my finger and touch it to the roof of the car or the doorway of the plane," Padalecki admits. "I don't know why. I think someone said it was good luck when I was growing up. And I do this thing called the 'Texas Tap'. Whenever I toast with somebody, whether we're having a beer, a glass of wine, a shot, or even water, I'll clink glasses and then I'll tap the table or tap something, and if I'm standing, then I'll tap the back of my hand. I also like things being on an even number. If the volume is at 33, I'll turn it to 34 or 32, and if the air conditioning is on 65 degrees, I'd rather it be on 66 or 64. I don't know what all that means, but I consider it good luck."

A Closer Look At:
CHANGELINGS

"Changelings occur in several different mythologies in Europe and Asia," notes Phil Sgriccia. "There's a lot of lore about a creature coming into your house and stealing your baby and leaving a fake baby, a wooden baby, or their own baby," adds Sera Gamble. The perpetrators can be any sort of magical creature, ranging from selkies (creatures that looks like seals, but can shed their skin to look human) to fairies, elves, and trolls, which are the most common.

The motivations for the baby swap are as varied as the creatures that take part in this terrifying practice. The most common is that some fairy folk derive their magic from demons and must pay their debt by sacrificing one of their own children, so they sacrifice a human child instead while their child is safely raised by humans. Some want human slaves, some want to experience the love of a human child, some think humans will raise their children better, and some just like the taste of young humans…

DEAN: We'll just bust in, drag the kids out, torch them on the front lawn. That'll play *great* with the neighbors.

"The original lore about changelings is that they're babies," Eric Kripke points out, "not older children like they are in 'The Kids Are Alright'. We just couldn't quite bring ourselves to have Sam and Dean take blowtorches to infants."

In folk tales, changelings are often discovered because they have voracious appetites, horrible tempers, and other extremely unpleasant traits. "They're just not your sweet perfect baby that has your genetics," Gamble explains. "That's off in fairyland. But being who we are, we had to make them chomp on the back of your neck and suck out all your spinal fluid.

"In the lore they're not called 'changeling parents', they're goblins and fairies and trolls, but we don't talk about fairies very much on *Supernatural*… except disparagingly when somebody talks about a creature that Dean is sure doesn't exist. He's like, 'Yeah, fairies and unicorns…'"

Regardless of whether it's fairies, trolls, or monstrous supernatural "changeling parents" trying to steal your child, the best way to protect your children is to put iron under their mattresses. But if it's too late, and the swap's already been made, what you need to know is that the real children are usually stashed underground somewhere, and the only way to rid yourself of the life-sucking changeling children is to set them on fire.

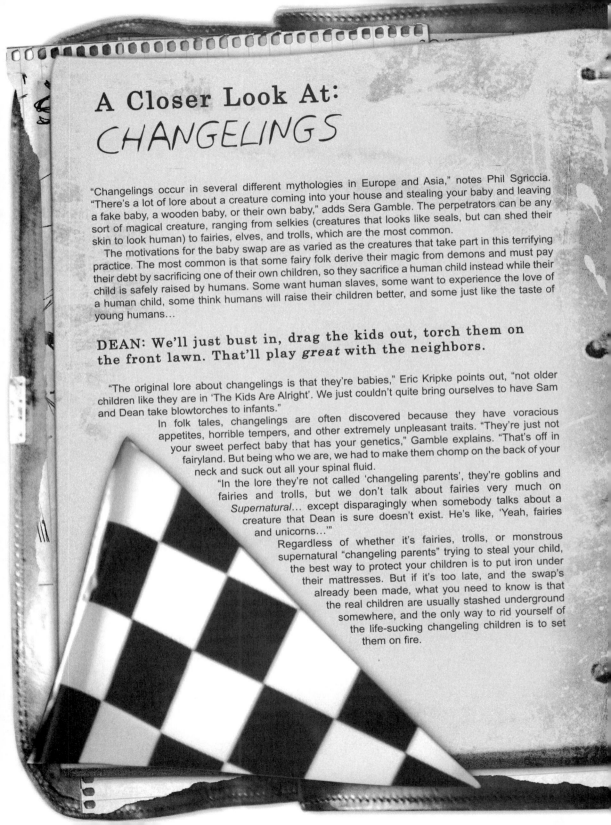

A Closer Look At:
CURSED CHARMS

"What's weird is we needed a good luck object and the rabbit's foot occurred to me," Ben Edlund reveals, "but I was thinking of that pink dyed rabbit's foot you get on a museum fieldtrip. Then we looked it up and it's very storied with hoodoo lore of how you prepare it."

Not any rabbit's foot will do. It has to be the left hind foot of a rabbit captured in a graveyard during a full or new moon. And while you need to shoot the rabbit with a silver bullet (or stab it with a silver knife), you must be careful not to kill it instantly, for its blood should still be flowing when you cut off its foot.

"It's a pretty powerful piece of magic lore," notes Edlund. "We're really lucky, because it grounded something whimsical in real history. Then we cursed it. I've known people who, if they ever lost their lucky charm, it was traumatic — they were waiting for bad luck, since they'd lost their shield against it. So that felt like a pretty good extension of the lore. We tend to take the familiar supernatural thing and make it as toxic as possible, as dangerous to humans as we can."

"Our rabbit's foot is not the kind you get on a little keychain," Bob Singer points out, "ours is a bigger, ugly, screwed up rabbit's foot."

SAM: It's a hell of a luck charm.
BOBBY: It's not a luck charm! It's a curse. She made it to kill people, Sam. See, you touch it, you own it. You own it, sure, you get a run of good luck to beat the Devil. But you lose it, that luck turns. Turns so bad that you're dead inside a week.
SAM: Well, so I won't lose it, Bobby.
BOBBY: *Everybody* loses it!

"If there's any lore on curse boxes, I don't know it. I just made it up," Edlund declares. "It was based in a way on Pandora's Box. The boxes magically cut off the cursed items from the rest of the continuum. There might be things like that out there…"

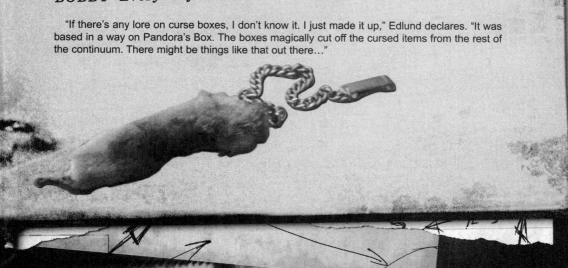

SIN CITY

Written by:
Robert Singer
and Jeremy
Carver

Directed by:
Charles Beeson

Guest Cast: Martin Papazian (Richie), Sasha Barrese (Casey), Elisa King (Cheryl), Matthew Harrison (Reggie Maynard), Todd Curran (John), Gregory Bennett (Cop), Dean Paul Gibson (Bartender), Gavin Buhr (Max), Don S. Davis (Trotter), Richard Keats (Andy Johnson), Robert Curtis Brown (Father Gil), Julia Anderson (Bar Woman), Phoebe Greyson (Nun)

Sam and Dean investigate a rash of violent deaths in Elizabethville, Ohio, a once-sleepy town that has been turned into a haven for gamblers and drinkers. It quickly becomes clear that demons have infiltrated the town and are using their powers of persuasion to make the townspeople succumb to their basic instincts.

The brothers meet up with Richie, a fun-loving hunter friend of Dean's, but Richie is soon murdered by Casey, a hot bartender who's possessed by a demon. Of course, it isn't long before Dean succumbs to Casey's charms and she takes him to a wine cellar in her house. She thinks she's lured another victim into her trap, but she finds herself stuck in a devil's trap instead because Dean was wise to her true intentions. The problem is, the demon's more powerful than Dean imagined, and she brings the roof down over the stairway, sealing Dean in with her.

Casey destroys Dean's exorcism book, but he figures it won't be long before Sam tracks him down. While they're waiting, the demon and demon hunter form an unexpected bond. Casey explains to Dean that demons have relationships, too. And in the same way as some humans believe in God, some demons have faith that Lucifer exists.

Meanwhile, Ruby helps Bobby rebuild the Colt, and Sam goes to the town priest to get information on Casey. All four of them arrive at Casey's place, where the priest attacks Sam and Bobby, revealing he's a demon, too. The priest clears a path into the cellar and attacks Dean. Casey begs him not to kill Dean, but Sam races in with the Colt and kills both demons, though it's obvious Dean wanted to just exorcise Casey. Dean's concerned that Sam could be turning into too cold a killer, but Bobby assures him Sam is fine.

CASEY: Guess you should have paid more attention in Latin class.
DEAN: I don't know what you're smiling about. You're not going anywhere.
CASEY: And apparently, neither are you.
DEAN: Yeah, but I got somebody coming for me, and he *did* pay attention in class.
CASEY: Oh, right, Sam. Everyone says he's the brains of the outfit.
DEAN: Everyone?

"For 'Sin City' I'd thrown out the idea of doing something based on the movie *Enemy Mine*, where an earthling and an alien are trapped together," reveals writer Jeremy Carver. "And [executive producer] Bob Singer was like, 'Oh, that's based on *Hell in the Pacific,'* an older movie about a Japanese and an American soldier trapped on an island during World War Two. At first they try to kill each other and then they have to start up a begrudging friendship. So that turned into, 'What would happen if Dean and a demon were trapped in a cave?'

"That was intimidating for my first script, because I realized that meant that for the second half of the script they're going to be trapped in a room together with little action and very heavy mythology about demons. I could not have written that, not successfully, because it was too much of an unknown chunk of mythology."

Singer agreed that "the conversation between Dean and the demon was a little too much for a brand-new writer to take on, so we decided I'd write it with Jeremy. Basically he did the first part and I did the second part, and that's all very much in my wheelhouse. This genre is not something I'm totally comfortable with writing. The stuff that Eric writes, I can't, so most of the writing I do on the show is character stuff and internal workings of scenes.

"Everybody likes to ask, 'What is your favorite scene in *Supernatural?* I love the

Above
Sam stares Ruby down.

DID YOU KNOW?

The bar from 'The Magnificent Seven' was reworked to become the 'Sin City' bar.

Above

Sam's taking no chances.

scene in 'Faith', where at the end of the show Dean says to the girl, 'I don't pray, but I'll pray for you,'" reveals Singer, "whereas Eric's favorite moment was when the guy's sticking his hand down the garbage disposal. So you put the things we cherish together and you end up with a pretty complete show."

DEAN: Azazel...?
CASEY: What, you think his friends just called him "Yellow-Eyes"? He had a name.

"It was a real pleasure getting to write with Bob," Carver attests. "He's very economical in thought. Reading a page of dialogue from someone like him, who's been doing it for a while, is much different from reading from someone who hasn't. It's very sparse and gets right to it with as few words as possible. Working with him was a lot of fun."

"I really liked that they have a conversation about demonism," Singer points out. "We get the demon's point of view in a very considered and methodical sort of way. The way demons feel about what's good, what's fair... Just sort of humanizing it, giving the other side of the argument."

Constructing the scene that trapped Dean with the demon was not an easy task. "There was a lot of talk about that wine cellar set," notes production designer John Marcynuk. "The ceiling collapsing was not an easy gag to do. We were literally working up until the hour to finish off that set and dress it properly.

"There were a lot of challenges with that main street too, because we didn't have

MUSIC

'Run Through The Jungle' by Creedence Clearwater Revival

'Bad Seed' by Brimstone Howl

'Nikki' by Sasquatch

'Did You See It' by Mother Superior

control over the street itself and there was actual traffic going by, so we were only using part of it."

Location manager Paul Lougheed adds, "That was a hectic day in the city of Langley, which has always been over-filmed as it is. Some film companies do it right and some of them do it wrong. I went into a café and overheard the number one grump in the neighborhood say how good our crew was compared to others."

Marcynuk goes on to explain that "because this town was supposed to be sort of a New Orleans/Las Vegas hybrid brought to a small town, the motel rooms in that episode were a little more flamboyant, more Las Vegas; the color scheme was old Las Vegas." Costume designer Diane Widas carried that over into the clothes the townsfolk wore. "Passion colors — purples and oranges and reds — were brought into the mix to create that 'anything goes' feeling; psychologically bring that out in you." ✎

BEDTIME STORIES

Written by:
Cathryn Humphris

Directed by:
Mike Rohl

Guest Cast: Derek Lowe (EMT), Mary Black (Grandma), Victoria Duffield (Little Red), Tracy Spiridakos (Callie), Libby Osler (Cinderella), Peter Jenkins (Attending Doctor), Patrick Gilmore (Ken), Sandra McCoy (Crossroads Demon), Maxine Miller (Elderly Lady), Malcolm Scott (Kyle), Michael Coleman (Jack), Chris Cochrane (Edmund), Ava Hughes (Snow White/Young Callie), Aron Eastwood (Wolf), Kimberley Warnat (Julie), Christopher Cousins (Dr. Garrison)

A string of strange murders brings Sam and Dean to Maple Springs, New York, and they're perplexed to discover that the crimes resemble fairy tales, such as the Three Little Pigs (three chubby house builders are attacked by a man that acts like a wolf), Hansel and Gretel (a couple hiking in the woods are fed treats by a kindly old woman who wants to kill and eat them), and Cinderella (a girl's stepmother shackles and beats her).

It soon becomes clear that the 'Snow White' in their midst — a girl named Callie, trapped in a coma for years after being poisoned by her stepmother — is responsible. Hovering at a point of existence that's near death, she's able to detach her spirit from her body, and with practice she's learned to control other people. She uses a 'Big Bad Wolf', in the form of a regular guy, to go after 'Little Red Riding Hood'... Dean manages to save Little Red and Sam acts as ghost whisperer to Callie, allowing her to talk to her father and tell him what happened to her. Then Callie lets go, her body dies, and she moves on.

That night, while Dean sleeps, Sam summons the Crossroads Demon and threatens to kill her with the remade Colt unless she releases Dean from his deal. She informs him that she's just the saleswoman, a middleman for a much more powerful demon. When she refuses to tell Sam who her boss is, he shoots her anyway... eliminating their one lead to the demon who holds Dean's contract.

SAM: I'm here to make you an offer.
CROSSROADS DEMON: *You're* going to make me an offer? That's adorable.
SAM: You can let Dean out of his deal, right now. He lives... *I live...* you live. Everyone goes home happy. Or... you stop breathing, permanently.

"In 'Bedtime Stories', I got to work with Sandra McCoy, who played the Crossroads Demon, which was really cool and interesting," shares Jared Padalecki. "We met on [the movie] *Cry_Wolf*, so it was fun to come full circle after four years and work together again. But it was sort of a crazy night of filming, because we were out there in the freezing cold, and she was in this little dress and here I am in all my jackets and thermals — and she couldn't have any of that because she was in a dress. I felt

bad for her."

"I was trying to act like, 'Oh, it's fine,' but really I was so miserable," confesses McCoy. "That dress was almost non-existent and it was freezing, but I was determined to be professional. Usually, if you're freezing, in between takes one of the wardrobe assistants will run over with a huge jacket and put it around you and you can sit near the heater until they yell 'Action' again, but I insisted I didn't need it. I figured I'd get used to the cold, like jumping into water, but it never happened. My teeth chattered so much that my jaw was sore for a week after that."

McCoy also explains that while, of course, "I never actually got shot by [Jared]," the nature of the stunt at the end of the scene meant, "I had to fake throwing my head back, so I just kinda stood there and gave myself whiplash!"

Nonetheless, both Padalecki and McCoy found the experience "a lot of fun,"

As fun as the experience was, McCoy divulges that acting with Jared did give her a major case of stage fright. "I was so nervous. I never even ran the scene with Jared until we got on set. When I was in his trailer fifteen minutes before shooting, I still couldn't run the lines with him. He and Jensen usually run their lines on the drive to work and then in one of their trailers just to get everything down, and I couldn't

Above

The Crossroads
Demon is amused by
Sam's threats.

even do it. So we ran the entire scene once with the director and the crew and they're like, 'Okay, great,' and I kept a smile on, but then as soon as I started walking away from set, I started bawling. Jared had to calm me down because I was just so nervous. I just couldn't stop crying, and nobody on set knows to this day that I was such a wreck. Everyone thought it was so fun for me, but it was harder to act like I was okay than it was to act like the Crossroads Demon! I needed to excuse myself and go to Craft Services every break so I could eat and cry like the emotional girl that I was that night."

DEAN: I'm gonna go stop the Big Bad Wolf. Which is the weirdest thing I've ever said.

"Sandy's so sweet," Lauren Cohan confides. "She's one of those people where you think she can't really be this nice and then you speak to her more and you're like, 'Oh my God, she's amazing!'"

Another amazing aspect of this episode was the crew's ability to get across the fairy tale settings without going overboard. "We were always walking a thin line between fairy tale and reality," notes production designer John Marcynuk. "We couldn't be *too* fairy tale, yet it *was* a fairy tale. The highlight for me was Granny's cottage in the woods. Eric's instructions were that it couldn't be too much of a gingerbread house, [so] we made it a more cottage style, and it really looked good out there when you came upon it in the woods." Locations manager Russ Hamilton says "it's interesting because it was just a trail with a gravel road in the park, and three days later there's a cottage built there and the greens department has greened it in — you would think it'd been there hundreds of years. Everyone's always amazed with how quickly we can take things down too. Literally within a matter of hours sometimes you would never even know the film crew was there."

Below
Sam doesn't hesitate
to shoot the
"smartass" Crossroads
Demon.

A Closer Look At:
FAIRY TALES

Once upon a time there were two brothers, one a charming knight on a black steed and the other a friendly giant. They roamed from village to village, slaying dragons, casting out demons, unmasking witches, and banishing restless spirits. Then one day they came upon Callie, a sleeping beauty with hair as black as night and skin as white as snow. They discovered that her stepmother had poisoned her with a magical potion and she was doomed to sleep for all eternity. Then the handsome princes kissed her, she awoke, and lived happily ever after.

At least, that's how the modern bedtime version ends.

In the original telling, passed down orally for centuries, the sleeping girl, a prisoner of her own mind, willed her spirit free, but was unable to convince her father that her ghost wasn't a figment of his imagination. And when she found her stepmother had already died, meaning she couldn't exact her revenge, she lost her mind and went on a violent killing spree! Isn't that sweet?

DEAN: What the hell do you make of that?
SAM: Actually, I do have a theory. Sorta.
DEAN: Hit me.
SAM: Well, I'm thinking about... fairy tales.
DEAN: Oh. That's... that's nice. You think about fairy tales often?

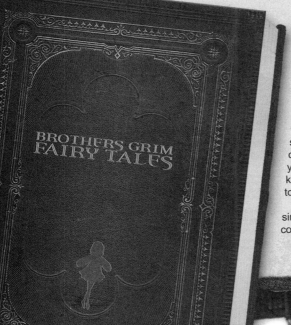

Generally speaking, a fairy tale is a story that features folkloric characters (including popular mainstays such as fairies, witches, goblins, trolls, and talking animals) and often magical or supernatural elements (such as fairy godmothers, magically cursed apples, and seeds that grow into giant beanstalks that take you to castles in the sky). All versions, ranging from horrifying tales of violence and cruelty to sweet tales of princesses and "fairy tale romances", were created to teach children and adults alike important life lessons. Take Little Red Riding Hood for example: Don't stray from the path to grandma's house (a symbol of virtue), or you'll wind up in a stranger's bed, which will lead to your destruction. For adults, the underlying message is clear, but children will be unlikely to see beyond the immediate story. And the moral in Hansel and Gretel is an early version of the warning not to take candy from a stranger... Then there's the Three Little Pigs, which is ostensibly about doing things right and taking pride in your work, because if you're lazy you won't be able to keep a roof over your head... and that, of course, will lead to a horrible death.

Fairy tales have been around in some form in all cultures since before recorded history, but particularly in the last couple of centuries, the sex and violence elements have

been toned down to reflect what adults feel is suitable to children's ears, resulting in the tamer versions we have in most picture books and movies today.

"Even in the Disney versions there's a lot of murder, a lot of missing or dead parents and children in peril though," Cathryn Humphris points out. "There are still a lot of allegorical elements of sex, and there's violence." Still, fairy tales don't seem on the surface to be an obvious fit for the *Supernatural* world...

"It was really fun to take them and turn them into something so nasty," Humphris enthuses. "Part of the fun just became, 'How can we make the elements work?' Obviously, with a lot of fairy tales there's magic — they are stories where the supernatural is used to get across real life lessons. The challenge was to have fairy tales feel very grounded and real. On the one hand, you have to let the audience know that you're referencing the Three Little Pigs, but on the other hand have them feel like these are three real men arguing about construction. Those things were a challenge."

DEAN: I thought those things ended with everyone living happily ever after?
SAM: No, no, not the originals. See, the Grimm Brothers' stuff was kind of like the folklore of its day, full of sex, violence, cannibalism. It got sanitized over the years, turned into Disney flicks and bedtime stories.
DEAN: So you think the murders are what? A re-enactment? That's a little crazy.
SAM: Crazy as what? Every day of our lives?
DEAN: Touché.

They solved that challenge by having a young girl's spirit cause the stories to play out in the real world. "There's a ghost called a 'fetch', which is the spirit of someone who's between death and life," notes Humphris. "Dean was a fetch [in 'In My Time of Dying'] and he was able eventually to move a glass," reminds Ben Edlund. "If you hover there long enough, you get some kind of control." Callie had years of practice before she took control of the 'Big Bad Wolf'...

Some people believe you don't have to be in a coma or near death in order to detach your spirit from your body, or *astral project*. It supposedly just takes lots of concentration. "I've read the books, and I've tried," Edlund confesses. "I'm not a very good astral projector." Then again, maybe it's not such a great idea to leave your body. "It's spooky because then you have to get back." And what if you *can't* get back?

In other words, don't try this at home, kiddies.

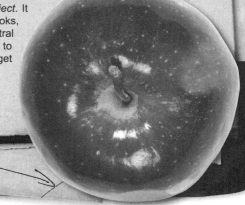

RED SKY AT MORNING

Written by:
Laurence Andries

Directed by:
Cliff Bole

Guest Cast: Steve Archer (Security Guard), Tobias Slezak (Todd Warren), Michael Denis (Waiter), Steve Lawlor (Ghost Captain), Robert Moloney (Peter Warren), Ellen Geer (Gertrude Case), Peter Grier (Ghost Sailor), Samantha Simmonds (Sheila)

Sam and Dean investigate a rash of weird dry-land drownings, preceded by sightings of a ghost ship. Before they can uncover the identity of the vengeful spirit, they run into Bela, who says she is working for Gertrude Case, the elderly aunt of one of the victims. She warns them to stay out of her way, but there's no chance in hell that'll happen.

That night, a man drowns at home, and Sam and Dean learn that his brother, Peter, also saw the ghost ship. Peter refuses their protection, then drowns in his car. Bela reveals she's actually there for an occult item. A sailor, hung for treason by his own brother, had his hand removed post mortem, creating a Hand of Glory — said to unlock any door — which is currently on display at a local maritime museum.

Gertrude obtains invitations for them all for a function at the museum, and while Sam reluctantly keeps Gertrude, who has a penchant for attractive young men, occupied, Dean and Bela steal the Hand of Glory. Bela tricks Dean, then runs off and sells the Hand. The ghost ship then appears to her, so she turns to the brothers for help. They have deduced that each victim was involved in the death of a family member, but Bela refuses to discuss her parents' deaths.

At the sailor's grave, Sam summons the ghost's brother, which distracts the vengeful spirit from killing Bela. The ghost hurls himself at his brother and the spirits merge in a watery explosion, then vanish. Bela thanks the brothers by giving them $10,000. Sam gets pissed off when Dean suggests Atlantic City, appearing to care more about playing craps than giving a crap that he's going to die.

DEAN: What a crazy old broad.
SAM: Why, because she believes in ghosts?
DEAN: Look at you, sticking up for your girlfriend. You cougar hound.
SAM: Bite me.
DEAN: Hey, not if she bites you first.

Consulting producer Laurence Andries shares his inspiration for 'Red Sky at Morning': "The idea came from, 'What if we do the Kennedy curse? A rich family where people were dying.' That felt too aristocratic and too removed from the audience though. Then the Kennedys got me thinking about the eastern seaboard and that got me onto ghost ships. See how the brain twists and turns? Then that train of thought took me to the episode you saw.

DID YOU KNOW?

The cemetery at the end of the episode was built at Heritage Park in Burnaby, BC, the same location as the Elderly Lady's cottage in 'Bedtime Stories'.

Above
Dean has the Hand of
Glory in his sights.

"My conception for the teaser was a big elaborate set-piece where she feels water dripping on her forehead from the ceiling. She goes up to the bathroom and the entire floor's filled with water, like the flood in *The Shining*. And that's when she meets her end. But when we get the budget report back on a script, we go, 'Alright, what's Plan B?' We write our dreams and shoot our realities."

Even Plan B didn't work out. "We had to do so much to wrestle it down to budget," bemoans creator Eric Kripke. "We'd written these very cool drowning deaths, which was kind of our raison d'être for this episode. The girl was supposed to get locked in the shower and the shower literally fills to the top and she drowns. When the guy was locked in the car, the car was supposed to fill all the way up with water and we see him drown. We were really excited about those set-pieces, but we couldn't afford them, so it became the big wet spook touching them on the shoulder and then everyone spits water and they're dead."

"Likewise," adds Andries, "the party was a much bigger affair in my head and in my first couple of drafts. That would've cost a trillion dollars, so that went out the window. I wanted to put Sam and Dean in a situation they'd never been in before, so to have them in Hugo Boss suits at a very fancy affair was something that they'd never really done."

"Bela went and paid for the suits and got the boys all decked out," costume designer

Diane Widas explains. "There's no bargain basement there. Even in their FBI looks, they're not quite as bargain basement as they used to be; the suits fit them a little better than they used to. Plus, Lauren Cohan was a lovely girl, so pretty much anything looked good on her. It was just a matter of finding something that flattered her and made her look elegant and that she felt hot in and everybody liked."

SAM: How do you sleep at night?
BELA: In silk sheets, rolling naked in money. Really, Sam, I expect the attitude from him. But you?
SAM: You shot me!
BELA: I barely grazed you. Cute, but a bit of a drama queen, yeah?

Cohan didn't feel particularly elegant during the final scene of the episode. "That one was actually the most difficult and the most gruelling, in terms of being dramatic and getting to use all different kinds of effects, and stuff that I hadn't previously done," she notes. "They had this contraption where I had to vomit the water. That was pretty hard."

Toby Lindala, head of special effects makeup, enjoyed building that contraption. "It was fun. We all had a chance to wear the rig in the shop here — a tube just rigged to a denture on the off-camera side type of thing — and we got a real large volume

of water coming out…"

The visual effects department also had a lot of fun on 'Red Sky at Morning'. "That was a really big episode for us," comments visual effects coordinator Ivan Hayden. "It started out where we were going to do the big boat shots, but then in the teaser, when the jogger looks up and sees the ghost ship, the reaction she gave — 'Did I just see what I thought I saw?' — gave us a cool direction to go in. We came up with the idea of doing the lightning rather than showing, 'Oh look, there's the ship in creepy fog coming across the water.' Instead, we got to play it with more lightning, making it visible only in lightning strikes. That drew it out a little bit and gave a creepy feel to it.

"For the scene where the ghost brothers collide into each other, we had a second unit day where we just popped water balloons and threw water at a thousand frames a second. So we're turning that second of time into a prolonged moment that allows us to hesitate it. It starts regular motion, and as the ghosts collide, things go into slow motion. So you get to see the water erupt in that beautiful way. We shot all of those elements, then we brought it into the computers and created actual 3D water elements. We modelled our characters and turned them into water and rammed them into each other, applied the textures on top of it so it looked real, and then we combined the live action water balloons with the 3D and the live action plates. It came off really well, and it's one of my favorite shots of our show so far." ✐

DID YOU KNOW?

The high society ball was filmed at the same location as the hotel in season two's 'Playthings'.

FRESH BLOOD

Written by:
Sera Gamble

Directed by:
Kim Manners

Guest Cast: Matthew Humphreys (Dixon), Mercedes McNab (Lucy), Katie Chapman (Girl), Jon Kralt (Young Man), Natalia Minuta (Blonde #2), Daniella Evangelista (Blonde #1), Damon Johnson (Man), Clare Elliott (Blondie), Aliyah O'Brien (Beautiful Woman)

Gordon escapes from prison and bribes Bela to get Sam's location. Sam and Dean are in Albany, New York, where they capture a female vampire who claims not to know how she became a vampire. The boys discover that a vampire named Dixon is offering his blood as a trendy new drug to girls at a nightclub. They stop Dixon from feeding his next victim, but the vampire bolts. Before Sam and Dean can give chase, they're shot at by Gordon and Kubrick. Dean draws their fire, but only Kubrick pursues him. Then before he can chase Sam, Gordon is knocked out by Dixon.

Gordon wakes up in Dixon's lair, where two newly-turned female vampires are chained up. Gordon's barrage of insults causes Dixon to change his mind about feeding Gordon to the girls, and he infects Gordon with his "filthy disease" instead.

Figuring out Bela sold them out, Dean calls her and threatens to kill her. Not liking people holding grudges against her, she uses a "talking board" to contact a spirit and learns Gordon's location — but Gordon's already gone. Vampire Gordon visits Kubrick and promises to kill himself after Sam is taken care of, but Kubrick attempts to kill him, so Gordon rips his heart out.

Dean tries to go after Gordon on his own, but Sam tells Dean he's sick of his kamikaze act. Dean agrees that they'll stick together and go after Gordon in the morning. But Gordon lures them out with a captive young woman. The brothers try to rescue her, but become trapped and separated. Dean kills the newly-turned vampire hostage with the Colt while Sam battles the turbo-charged Gordon. Dean distracts Gordon long enough for Sam to decapitate him with barbed wire.

SAM: You know what, man? I'm sick and tired of your old stupid kamikaze trick.
DEAN: Whoa, whoa... Kamikaze? I'm more like a ninja.
SAM: That's not funny.
DEAN: It's a little funny.
SAM: No, it's not.

Fans of *Buffy the Vampire Slayer* and *Angel* received a pleasant surprise when Mercedes McNab, who played the vampire Harmony on those *Supernatural* predecessors, appeared in 'Fresh Blood' as Lucy — a vampire! Question is, does McNab have any concerns about being typecast? "I was a bit trepidatious about Lucy because I had to play another vampire, but I loved working with [executive producer] Kim

Manners so much on *The Adventures of Brisco County Jr.* that I just thought, 'Do it!'

"Harmony was such a different kind of character than Lucy too," McNab points out. "Lucy was serious and more dramatic, whereas Harmony was kind of comic relief. For Lucy, I put myself in that situation as if I'd woken up and someone had kidnapped me and I didn't remember the events of the night before.

"It's always weird going on to something as a guest star," states McNab, "but Kim was super, he just made me feel comfortable and at home. And Jared and Jensen were super nice. They were really generous actors… and not too hard on the eyes!"

Sterling K. Brown didn't share screen time with McNab, but had the pleasure of working with Lauren Cohan. "Lauren was an absolute sweetheart. Our scene together was one of my favorites. I like the character; she's a little different."

But not as different as Kubrick is from Gordon. "I always wondered how those two individuals got together."

"Sterling and I went over that," Michael Massee reveals, "and we decided that we'd known each other for quite some time and I was his right hand man, somebody he could count on." Brown adds, "Kubrick is well-meaning, and a sweet guy. When I was watching the episode with my wife, she looked at me and screamed, 'Why did you do that? I can't believe you killed him!' It definitely evoked a visceral response from her.

"It was hard to be a vampire because up to that point, whatever people might have said about Gordon, I considered him to be ultimately good. For him, the ends justified

Above

Sam cautiously hunts vampire Gordon.

the means. Once he became a vampire, it was harder than I could have imagined. That being said, it's always more fun to be bad than good."

Perhaps an even bigger challenge than going from good to bad is trying to portray someone who is inherently bad as good. "Dixon is a deeply misunderstood vampire," states Matthew Humphreys. "Someone at odds with how to create a family in his reality. The fascination for me was that it was so easy to rationalize what he did. There was no evil motive behind it, and so it really unhinged that notion that vampires are mindless, bloodthirsty animals." Hopefully Humphreys will get to play Dixon again, because there was no indication that the brothers killed him. "I want to believe that Dixon is out there!" Humphreys enthuses.

"Gordon's demise was great," proclaims Jared Padalecki. "We got to see the darker side of Sam when he decapitated him with pure hatred. It wasn't like Sam had been holding off, saying, 'I know he's trying to kill me, but he might be right…' It was, 'You know what? He's a vampire! He's killing people; it's time for him to go.' It was a fun fight scene."

"I really lucked out," notes Sera Gamble. "I wrote the first and last episodes with the character Gordon. I sat down with Eric and conceptualized this fanatical hunter, and by the end of his story arc he's become his own worst nightmare, he's turned into a monster. There's something so satisfying about turning him into a vampire and chopping his head off with razor wire! Sterling did a perfect job, as did Jared and Jensen."

"It was unfortunate to lose Gordon," says production designer John Marcynuk. "He

Above

Dean's definitely not happy about the "new" Gordon.

was a strong character. For his death scene, we tried to stick to mostly green tones and a cool color palette throughout, so that when you see the blood, there's that much more contrast. It just makes Gordon's death scene more jarring."

BELA: **What's so pressing about finding the boys, anyway?**
GORDON: **Sam Winchester's the Anti-Christ.**
BELA: **I heard something about that...**
GORDON: **It's true.**
BELA: **...from my good friend the Easter Bunny. Who heard it from the Tooth Fairy... Are you off your meds?**

Visual effects coordinator Ivan Hayden would've liked to have made the decapitation shot even more jarring. "It goes directly from Sam cutting Gordon's head off to looking at Gordon's head on the ground and there's no motion, so we created an animation with a bit of a head rock. Standards and practices wouldn't go for it though; it was a little too graphic."

"Sam basically garroting Gordon with razor wire is one of the coolest deaths we've ever had," creator Eric Kripke proclaims. "It's a good lesson in knowing if you come up with a cool idea that's effectively executed, the fact that it's illogical makes no difference to the viewer. We were like, 'Are we saying Sam is super-powered strong to be able to cut through somebody's spinal cord? How can he pull so hard to pop off Gordon's head and not pop off his own hands with the razor wire?' Excellent questions, but no one cares, because you want Gordon's head to pop off!" ✐

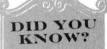

DID YOU KNOW?

Composer Chris Lennertz feels that "people associate the sound of violins with vampires. It's the connection with Eastern Europe and counts. So I made a conscious effort to steer away from woodwinds, brass, and piano, and went for a very violin-heavy score on 'Fresh Blood'."

A VERY SUPERNATURAL CHRISTMAS

Written by:
Jeremy Carver

Directed by:
J. Miller Tobin

Guest Cast: Spencer Garrett (Edward Carrigan), Colin Ford (Young Sam), Ridge Canipe (Young Dean), Merrilyn Gann (Madge Carrigan), Zak Ludwig (Eddie Carson), Don MacKay (Grandpa Carson), Emily Holmes (Melinda Walsh), Alex Bruhanski (Slimy Santa), Dryden Dion (Ronnie), Brandy Heidrick (Cheery Elf), Connor Levins (Jimmy Caldwell), Jennifer Copping (Cindy Caldwell), Douglas Newell (Mr. Siler), Victoria Bidewell (Molly Johnson)

It's Christmas time in Ypsilanti, Michigan, as Sam and Dean investigate a series of disappearances where victims were pulled up through chimneys. Dean wants to celebrate his last Christmas, but Sam refuses. He's unwilling to accept that Dean won't be around next year, and Christmas doesn't inspire happy memories for Sam. He recalls Christmas when he was eight, waiting to give his father a special gift, though it looked like John would be a no-show.

Sam and Dean suspect it's an Evil Santa (a.k.a. the Anti-Claus), but their best lead — a local professional Santa — doesn't pan out. Then a visit to the latest crime scene points them to Madge and Edward Carrigan, the seemingly harmless couple who made the meadowsweet wreaths owned by all the victims. The Carrigans are actually ancient pagan gods!

Another flashback to Christmas Eve 1991 reveals Sam reading his father's journal and learning that monsters are real... while Santa isn't. Disappointed when his father doesn't turn up, Sam gives Dean the gift, which turns out to be the amulet Dean wears to this day.

The boys sneak into the Carrigans' house and find human remains and the latest victim inside a sack in the basement. But Madge and Edward get the jump on them, then tie them to kitchen chairs. They prepare the Winchesters for the ritual sacrifice, extracting their blood and pulling out one of Sam's fingernails. Just as Edward is about to yank out one of Dean's teeth, a neighbor appears at the front door and the boys escape their bonds. A fight ensues, and the evil gods are eradicated by makeshift evergreen stakes torn from their Christmas tree.

Sam rethinks Christmas and decorates their motel room with a makeshift tree and ornaments. The boys drink rum and eggnog, exchange presents, avoid talking about their feelings, and watch a football game.

DEAN: So what the hell do you think we're dealing with?
SAM: Actually, I have an idea.
DEAN: Yeah?
SAM: It's gonna sound crazy...
DEAN: What could you possibly say that sounds crazy to me?
SAM: Um... Evil Santa?
DEAN: Yeah, that's crazy.

"I love eggnog!" Jensen Ackles enthuses. "In fact, that was really rum and eggnog we

DID YOU KNOW?

Despite the meticulous research that goes into *Supernatural*'s lore, Eric Kripke admits Sam got something wrong. "Sam said, 'Jesus was probably born in the fall.' That's not true. Jesus was probably born in the spring, which is why there are lambs in the manger — they're spring lambs."

were drinking in the scene. And we were both hammered. Just kidding! Eggnog was never a prevalent thing with my family, but when I got older and moved out to California, somebody pushed some out, and I was like, 'Yes! Where has this been?' It tastes like the holidays!"

Something else that tastes like the holidays is gingerbread, and the giant gingerbread house in the Carrigans' dining room looks good enough to eat, even if it is just set decoration. "For me, it's all about contrasts," explains production designer Jerry Wanek. "You've got the gods' home with that beautiful gingerbread house, everything is very festive, warm Christmas tones. Then you have the young boys in this little coal-burning old motel that is dank and they're alone.

"The two young actors were just incredible. They really pulled it off," states Wanek. "Not only did they make us believe they were young Sam and Dean," notes director J. Miller Tobin, "but they also carried off the emotional impact of being disappointed that their father doesn't show at Christmas, with that being the trauma that puts Sam off celebrating Christmas."

"Truth be told, the flashbacks were not in the original draft," confesses writer Jeremy Carver. "We had to add some page count, and it was actually Ben Edlund who came up with doing flashbacks, which added this whole new dimension to the episode.

"'A Very Supernatural Christmas' was a perfect blend of everything I like about this show, so it was an absolute joy to write," adds Carver. "The actress who played Madge Carrigan was great on *Everwood*, which is a show that my wife wrote for, and she's a very nice person, so I was tickled beyond belief that she was playing this

DID YOU KNOW?

In a random polling of *Supernatural* cast and crew, one hundred percent of respondents do not like Christmas fruitcake. Not counting Jensen Ackles, who's never tried it, but who feels that "judging from the stigma surrounding it, that's probably a good thing."

Above

Sam checks out the pagan gods' human meat grinder.

monster. She was fantastic! From writing to execution, she and [Spencer Garrett] fulfilled any dream that I could've had about writing for *Supernatural*."

"They were both brilliant," exclaims first assistant director Kevin Parks. "There's something about that sweet little couple turning out to be evil gods that's just hilarious," points out producer Sera Gamble. Costumer Diane Widas thinks it has something to do with the sweaters. "That was really fun because they wanted the sweaters to be very campy. When we first did Edward's sweater, it was even more over-the-top — we had 3D snowmen and stuff like that on it. We really just had a lot of fun being as frivolous about Christmas as absolutely possible."

> SAM: Well, we're not dealing with the Anti-Claus.
> DEAN: What'd Bobby say?
> SAM: That we're morons.

MUSIC

'Have Yourself A Merry Little Christmas' by Rosemary Clooney

'Silent Night' by Jensen Ackles & Jared Padalecki

The costumers also had fun with Santa and his elves. "Because the setting was a very tired little theme park, we gave the little elves ill-fitting costumes. We broke the costumes down so that they looked shabby, even though they were brand new. And because 'Bad Santa' was a drunk, we really made him look grungy."

"As a layer of his Bad Santa personality, we did a bulletin board for him," shares graphic designer Lee Anne Elaschuk, "where he tacked up all of his Christmas cards and artwork from the kids that sat on his lap. And some autographs from stars of the adult video industry. He'd also had some trips to Mexico, so we Photoshopped scenes of Santa doing tequila shooters in the bar and having a good time. I love that bulletin

board so much… and I don't think it was in the episode, but the actor saw it and that helped him to pull into his character."

"The art department did a brilliant job making everything completely insanely over-the-top Christmas," states Tobin. As co-executive producer Phil Sgriccia puts it, "We really twisted Christmas up good." ✷

Above
Sam and Dean exchange Christmas gifts.

The Spirit Of
Chri...

TO SAM & DEAN

WE WISH YOU A
MERRY CHRISTMAS,
WE WISH YOU A
MERRY CHRISTMAS...
HOPE YOU'RE DEAD
BY NEW YEAR!

BEST CHRISTMAS WISHES
EDWARD & MADGE CARRIGAN

DEAR CHUCKLEHEADS,

YOU'RE GETTING NOTHIN' FOR
CHRISTMAS. MOMMY AND DADDY ARE
DEAD. YOU'RE GETTING NOTHIN' FOR
CHRISTMAS, 'CAUSE YOU AIN'T BEEN
NOTHIN' BUT BAD'

YOUR PAL,
TRICKSTER.

WINCHESTERS

YOU BETTER WATCH OUT. BETTER COVER
YOUR TRACKS. HOPE NO ONE SELLS YOU
OUT. 'CAUSE I'M BREATHING DOWN YOUR
NECKS. HENRIKSEN IS COMING TO TOWN.
HENRIKSEN IS RUNNING YOU DOWN?
I'M MAKING A LIST. CHECKING IT TWICE.
GONNA FIND OUT WHERE THE NAUGHTY
ARE HIDING. – OKAY. SO I'M NO POET.
BUT GUESS WHAT? I DON'T NEED TO BE
TO LOCK YOUR ASSES UP. NEVER MIND
CHRISTMAS CAROLS. SOON YOU BOYS WILL
BE SINGING THE PRISON BLUES...

AGENT VICTOR HENRIKSEN

Peace
on earth

A Closer Look At:
GHOST SHIPS

"We tried to tap into the lore of ghost ships," Eric Kripke explains, "everything from the *Flying Dutchman* to the S.S. *Violet* and the *Griffon*. True lore about empty ships floating around the ocean."

Legend has it that the captain of the *Flying Dutchman* refused to back down from a fierce storm that kept him from rounding the Cape of Good Hope. Just before he and his crew perished, he swore that he'd keep sailing until Judgment Day if he had to. And apparently a demonic force — or perhaps the Trickster — took his vow at face value, since the ghost ship has been sailing the seas ever since.

SAM: I gotta I.D. the boat.
DEAN: Shouldn't be too hard. I mean, how many three-mast clipper ships have wrecked off the coast?
SAM: I checked that too, actually. Over one hundred and fifty.
DEAN: Wow.
SAM: Yeah.
DEAN: Crap.

The S.S. *Violet* was lost during a savage storm in the 1800s. Since then, the ship has sometimes been seen drifting at sea, but by the time rescuers drop lifeboats and attempt to come to her aid, the ship has vanished from sight.

In 1679, the *Griffon* mysteriously disappeared without a trace from Lake Michigan. The ship was never found, but numerous sailors have seen the ghostly ship, dubbing it the "Ghost Ship of the Great Lakes".

"Throughout history there's been mentions of these ships that, when you see them, they vanish on the horizon, and they're death omens — portents of your impending doom. If you see the ship, then the ghost comes after you and you die," states Kripke ominously.

"The notion of the hanged man's hand being chopped off and made into a Hand of Glory, that's a real thing," Kripke contends. "A Hand of Glory is an occult item that is very rare, very valuable, and it really is the hand of a hanged man. It has the power to open any locked door, which is what makes it so valuable. You could use it to rob banks, you could use it to get into anywhere you wanted to…"

A Closer Look At:
THE WINTER SOLSTICE PAGAN GOD

Christmas is a Christian holiday that celebrates the birth of Jesus Christ. A major part of Christmas tradition includes decorating Christmas trees, gift-giving, and stringing enough Christmas lights to blind your neighbors. And, of course, there's Santa Claus, a magical man who rides through the sky on a reindeer-drawn sled and drops down chimneys to deliver presents to children. In modern times, these traditions — often minus the worship of Jesus — have been co-opted by the masses, which could be considered to be ironic given that Christians themselves co-opted most of the traditions from the pagan winter solstice celebrations that predated Jesus's birth.

"The things our research bore out were fascinating," says Eric Kripke. "The god that we ended up finding was Hold Nickar, this pagan god who travels by flying sled, wears red with fur trim, comes over the winter solstice, and evergreens were used to worship him. There's just only a hop, skip, and a jump to Old Nick!"

DEAN: So you think we're dealing with a pagan god?
SAM: Yeah. Probably Hold Nickar, god of the winter solstice.
DEAN: And all these Martha Stewart wannabes buying these fancy wreaths...
SAM: Yeah, it's pretty much like putting a neon sign on your front door saying, "Come kill us."

"The main point is that Jesus wasn't born anywhere near December 25th. In order to spread Christianity, it was much easier for the church to say to the masses, 'You don't have to give up your holiday, because as luck has it, Jesus was born on that day, so celebrate the same thing. Just celebrate it as Jesus's birthday, not as the winter solstice festival. How does that change your life at all? Just accept the church.'

"When you stop to think about it, it makes no sense — Christmas trees, mistletoe, this giant red man who comes down your chimney and gives you presents... You do all of these strange rituals, yet what does any of that have to do with Jesus being born in the Middle East where there sure aren't a lot of evergreens? They just slapped a Christian name on them, and I'm surprised it isn't more common knowledge. It's fascinating real-life lore, and we were pleased to be able to make an episode about it."

Of course, the pagan gods don't find it fascinating; they've lost most of their worshippers, which drained their powers... but they're still powerful enough to carve you up like a Christmas turkey. Just don't mistake meadowsweet for mistletoe and you should be fine.

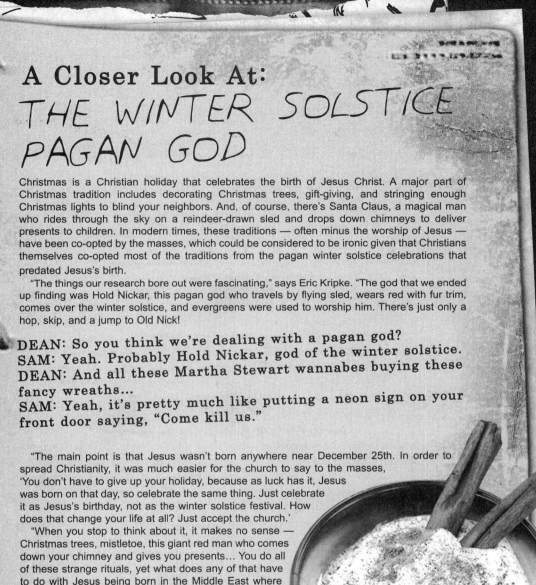

MALLEUS MALEFICARUM

Written by:
Ben Edlund

Directed by:
Robert Singer

Guest Cast: Rebecca Robbins (Amanda), Marisa Ramirez (Tammi Benton/Astaroth), Robinne Fanfair (Janet Dutton), Jonathan Watton (Paul Dutton), Erin Cahill (Elizabeth Clark), Kristin Booth (Renee Van Allen), Ken Tremblett (Ron)

When a healthy young woman's teeth fall out and she dies a mysterious death, Sam and Dean travel to Sturbridge, Massachusetts, where they discover black magic was involved. They save the victim's husband from choking to death on a maggot-infested hamburger and learn that he had an affair with a neighbor... a practicing witch, who the brothers find murdered next to a dead rabbit.

They determine that a coven of neighborhood witches are using witchcraft to make their suburban lives easier, but Ruby warns them to leave town because a very powerful demon's involved, who will surely kill them. Sam and Dean ignore her and, naturally, get on the head witch's bad side. She targets Dean, and when Sam can't do anything to help, he goes after the coven... only to discover that the head witch, Tammi, is possessed by the very demon that Ruby warned them about. Sam tries to shoot Tammi with the Colt, but she stops the bullet in mid-air, then throws Sam up against a wall with her demon force. She informs him that a new demon leader has arisen and wants Sam dead.

Meanwhile, Ruby rushes in and saves Dean, who is begrudgingly grateful. They go after Sam, but Tammi is more powerful than Ruby, having been the demon who turned Ruby into a witch and then brought her soul to Hell centuries ago. Surprisingly, Tammi has the power to exorcise other demons, but before she can fully rip Ruby from her body, Dean shoves Ruby's demon-killing knife into Tammi's back.

Later, Ruby tells Dean that all demons were human once, but that she's unusual because she retained her human memories. She also admits that she can't save him from Hell.

SAM: Look, I know it's dangerous, that *she's* dangerous... But like it or not, she's useful.
DEAN: No. We kill her before she kills us.
SAM: Kill her with what? The gun *she* fixed for us?
DEAN: Whatever works.
SAM: Dean, if she wants us dead, all she has to do is *stop saving our lives*.

Dean Winchester is constantly eating on *Supernatura*l, however, he'd surely draw the line at eating Paul Dutton's maggot-infested hamburger. But what about his real-life counterpart, Jensen Ackles? "Are you kidding me? I eat them all the time!" he proclaims. "It's the new McMaggot. You gotta check it out — it's awesome!"

Ackles is clearly joking, but key makeup artist Shannon Coppin is completely serious when she says, "there's a *maggot wrangler*. They keep them in a box on set all day, and it's enough to turn you off Craft Services for a while. They're really disgusting."

Creator Eric Kripke has never eaten a maggot burger either, but that scene was inspired by an incident from his life. "I opened my garbage can one day to find a dead possum in there," Kripke explains. "Every square millimeter of the can was coated in maggots, and it was so horrific. I was working on this story with Ben that day, and all I could think about were those maggots, and I said, 'We have to do a maggot scene, because that was one of the most horrific things I've ever seen.'"

"'Malleus Maleficarum' is the title no one can pronounce," bemoans co-executive producer Ben Edlund. "It's a book that was written in the Middle Ages, which was a guide for how to deal with witches. In essence, it was a weapon to be used against them."

"The title is a remnant from an earlier version of the story," Kripke reveals. "It started out where a small town suspects there's a witch among them and they create their own witch hunt. The reveal was going to be that a demon was causing various innocent women to look guilty and was manipulating the townsfolk into this paranoia and madness. We abandoned that because it felt too similar to 'Sin City', in which a demon manipulated humans to give in to their base impulses. So we said, 'Let's say there are real witches and the demon is one of them and manipulating them.' The story really came to life for us when we realized it was an opportunity to

Above

Dean and Sam agree to let Ruby take care of the dead bodies.

DID YOU KNOW?

Production designer Jerry Wanek reveals that "the cool Spanish-looking motel room was [inspired by] the Procol Harem song, 'Conquistador'."

tell Ruby's backstory. On top of that, my wife is in a book club, and I'm very suspicious of them because they never let any men in and I don't think they ever read the books they're supposedly talking about, so the idea of a witch coven disguised as a suburban book club was something that was entertaining to me."

RUBY: The answer is "yes", by the way.
DEAN: Sorry?
RUBY: Yes, the same thing will happen to you. Might take centuries, but sooner or later, Hell will burn away your humanity. Every Hell-bound soul, every one, turns into something else. Turns you into us. So, yeah... yeah, you can count on it.

Graphic designer Lee Anne Elaschuk found the setup entertaining, too. "We had to create a series of articles on the women — that Sam found online — and if you read them they're outrageous, but it amused me no end to work on them. Stories like, 'She had this really terrible cake, it's amazing she still won...' and 'She made this really basic quilt, how incredible she beat the entire crafting league and won the contest...'"

Marisa Ramirez enjoyed the premise as well. "Tammi comes across as this suburban housewife with these two perfect friends and they're all goody-goody and

then the husbands leave and they do their little rituals… and it was a lot of fun," she says. "But she was faking it the whole time, and Tammi's basically a badass, which I loved to play. I'd wanted to play a dark character for a long time, so it was easy for me to go there. I've been kickboxing for a long time, so I brought some natural ass-kicking to it. Katie Cassidy had been training too, so she knew what she was doing and it was like we were dancing together. It all flowed; it just worked out perfectly.

"I wouldn't mind having some sort of witch's powers," Ramirez muses. "It would be nice to get everything I wanted, but I don't know if I would pray to a demon for it. I might suffer for it in the end!" ✐

Above
Ruby comes off worst after her first confrontation with Astaroth.

HELL BROTH

Jensen Ackles has never eaten a maggot burger, but he did eat something that made him turn green… "Last year, I was in Japan at this nice restaurant and I ordered steamed clams in a spicy broth. So I'm motoring through 'em and I get to the last one and I had to pry it open and inside was this black slop. It smelled like someone had taken a spoon and scraped up some sewage and dropped it in there. As soon as I opened it, the whole table was like, *'Oh! What?'* And my girlfriend was like, 'You turned *green*.' I have a pretty iron stomach — I haven't thrown up in years — but I was [retching]. Obviously I didn't eat it, but I did eat the five surrounding it that soaked in the same broth. That'll go down in the record book as being one of the grossest things I've ever eaten."

MUSIC

'Every Rose Has It's Thorn' by Poison
'I Put a Spell On You' by Screamin' Jay Hawkins

DREAM A LITTLE DREAM OF ME

Written by: Cathryn Humphris, Sera Gamble

Directed by: Steve Boyum

Guest Cast: Katharine Isabelle (Ava Wilson), Richard De Klerk (Scott Carey), Bill Mondy (Dr. George Waxler), Levi James (Brady), Monique Ganderton (Biker Chick), Tom McBeath (Scott's Father), Jason Benson (Cop)

S am and Dean race to Bobby's side after he lapses into a coma. While unconscious, Bobby battles his personal demons, and it's revealed he became a hunter after killing his demon-possessed wife in self-defense. The brothers discover that a troubled college student, Jeremy, who's unable to dream due to brain damage caused by childhood beatings from his father, has ingested a magical root that allows him to enter other people's dreams... and when he kills people there, they die for real.

They contact Bela, who brings them some of the African dream root, which Dean places in a safe next to the Colt. Once Bela leaves, they take the root and enter Bobby's dream. They convince Bobby to wake up, but now the dreamwalker wants *all* of them dead. They can't find Jeremy in the real world and can't stay awake forever, so Dean goes to sleep and Sam takes more dream root to enter Dean's dream.

Jeremy arrives and ties Sam to the ground. Dean confronts his doppelganger, who tells him he's just his father's soldier, that no one will care if he goes to Hell and that he can't escape what he's going to become: a demon. Jeremy hammers away at the immobile Sam with a baseball bat, but Sam's able to manipulate the dream, too, and brings in Jeremy's father, who distracts him long enough for Sam to kill him with the bat.

They return to their motel to discover Bela's stolen the Colt. As they drive off, Dean admits that he doesn't want to die, and Sam promises they'll find a way to save him.

SAM: One problem, though. We're fresh out of African dream root. So unless you know someone who can score some...
DEAN: Crap.
SAM: What?
DEAN: Bela...
SAM: Bela? *Crap!*

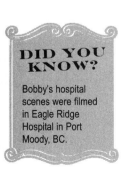

DID YOU KNOW?

Bobby's hospital scenes were filmed in Eagle Ridge Hospital in Port Moody, BC.

"We started with 'Dream a Little Dream' going a lot darker," reveals writer Cathryn Humphris. "In the original teaser, Bobby had children and was having dinner with his family. He looked up and saw blood pouring from one of his children's necks. And as he watched, all of their throats were supernaturally slit. As they were bleeding, they were saying, 'Why, daddy, why did you let this happen?' Ultimately, though, starting there made it really hard to figure out where to go next.

Above
Bobby's kitchen…
back when it still had
a woman's touch.

"I love writing Bobby, so I was excited when we decided to put him in the episode. For a long time we'd been throwing around this idea of 'How did Bobby become a hunter?' I'd pitched a version where Bobby was an expert at exorcisms because of a failed exorcism. Plus, we always knew his backstory would be grounded in family. It made sense to work that into the dream episode."

"Jim Beaver is a mountain of professionalism," remarks Jared Padalecki. "There's a scene where he's in the hospital bed telling us what's going on. It was just a shot of his face and his feet were right there in front of me, so as he was talking I was grabbing his toe and squeezing it as hard as I could because I was trying to get him to laugh. He kind of got a funny look on his face for a second… and then he played it off. But right as they called cut, he was like, 'What the hell is wrong with you?' I made myself laugh more than I made him laugh, but it's still my life's goal to get Jim Beaver on camera — and it's going to be on the gag reel!"

Something that did make the gag reel was Lauren Cohan laughing in bed with Jared Padalecki. "I'd heard whispers about that before we shot it," he reveals, "and I thought it was going to be a full-on love scene, so I was like, 'That's strange. She's been in three episodes and now I'm having a love scene with her?' I wasn't expecting Sam and Bela to be love interests, because earlier in the season she'd been more

THE
Aviary
HOTEL

Birdnest Lounge & Restaurant

PITTSBURGH, PA

★ ★ ★
CERTIFIED

Above

A postcard from the motel Sam and Dean stay at while in Pittsburgh. Wish you were here?

involved with Dean and I'd been more involved with Ruby. But then I read the script and laughed."

Producer Sera Gamble adds, "That dream sequence was just a place to have a little fun. I don't think of it as serious at all."

Since the episode revolved around dream sequences, the rest of them had to be taken very seriously. "The transition from dream to awake was really nice to achieve," comments director of photography Serge Ladouceur. "I took some liberties with colors too. The way I light things, I normally wouldn't use the full blue lights, I'd normally go for half blue light, but in the dream scenes I lit the background with full blue spots, and I carried the concept of that into the corridor because you're going from forest to hallway. Also, we used a long lens that compresses the background, so we took great care in making it a seamless transition."

"All the transitioning and the saturation of the color worked incredibly well visually," comments production designer Jerry Wanek.

"Same with the transfer from their motel room into Bobby's set," asserts art director John Marcynuk. "We took a wall from the motel room and put it in Bobby's set, started on that then panned across and you were in Bobby's set. And then for the reverse we put the fireplace wall back in. I felt that was fairly seamless."

"Jared threw his back out," director Steve Boyum reveals of shooting the baseball bat attack. "And that night we had [G. Michael Gray] just kick the hell out of Jared on the ground. He was really hurting, but he toughed it out. He went that extra mile to make Sam the most realistic character he can be." Of course, Boyum utilized Padalecki's stunt double, Michael Carpenter, as much as possible. "I took a beating from the bat on that one," Carpenter recalls. "The actor didn't hold back, either!" ▨

BOBBY: Before I knew it was him, he offered me a beer. I drank it. Dumbest friggin' thing.
DEAN: Oh, I don't know. It wasn't *that* dumb...
SAM: Dean... You didn't?
DEAN: I was thirsty.
SAM: That's great! Now he can come after either one of you.

DREAM TEA RECIPE

3/4 inch piece of African dream root
1 tablespoon ground ginger
1 tablespoon cinnamon
1 teaspoon honey (or sugar)
1 uncontaminated piece of dreamer's DNA (hair, saliva, boogers, eyelashes, skin…)

Grind root with pestle and mortar, mix in ginger and cinnamon. Place ingredients in a mug and stir in one cup boiling water. Add in honey, stir, then let steep for two minutes. Add milk or cream to taste.
Drop in DNA.
It's recommended you enjoy this beverage in bed as you will fall asleep within seconds of finishing. Then it's off to Never Never Land. Sweet dreams!

Above

Bobby (Jim Beaver) is grateful for the Winchester brothers' help.

MUSIC

'Long Train Runnin'' by The Doobie Brothers
'Dream a Little Dream of Me' by The Mamas and The Papas

A Closer Look At:
WITCHES

Anyone can be a witch. Even you. You just have to be willing to get your hands — and your soul — a little bloody.

Witches are not supernatural creatures; they are humans who control supernatural forces through the casting of spells. There are many ways to cast spells, the most common being incantations, inscription of sigils on objects to give them magical properties, manipulation of effigies (or poppets or 'voodoo dolls') to affect others magically, the performance of physical rituals such as animal sacrifices (or dancing naked in a circle under the moonlight), the use of magical herbs for potions or talismans, and gazing at crystal balls (or mirrors or blades) for divination. Popular uses of spell casting include flight (broomsticks optional), clairvoyance (great for buying lotto tickets), glamours (usually to make a witch look young and beautiful), and murder from a distance.

Descriptions of witches can be found in ancient texts from cultures all around the world. The best information can be found in a witch's own 'Book of Shadows'. Most witches, particularly members of covens, have their own handwritten spell-books, which they've copied from one of the original books that have been passed down through the ages. These powerful tomes are written in human blood and bound in human flesh.

"I grew up reading a lot of stuff about the supernatural, and at one point was intent on becoming a witch myself," declares Ben Edlund, "but it turned out to be a little bit too involved and took too much time. I read a lot of books on magic and how things were prepared, including the notion of step magic, where things are left under people's paths and if they step over it, it gets them. That influenced the hex bags and how they function."

DEAN: I hate witches. They're always spewing their bodily fluids everywhere...
SAM: Pretty much.
DEAN: It's *creepy.* Y'know, it's downright unsanitary!

"I prefer magic that is bloodier than that wave-a-magic-wand crap," Eric Kripke explains. "I like magic that hurts you and costs something... and there's bleeding in bowls and sacrificing chickens. The thing we really liked about the witches was that they didn't have the same powers as demons, they couldn't just point and hurt you. It was about how the spells work and rituals and hex bags and killing the rabbit — the real tactile elements of witches. That to me feels real."

If you have more willpower than Edlund and are still interested in witchcraft, keep in mind that the going rate for channeling a demon's dark forces is your soul...

A Closer Look At:
DREAMWALKING

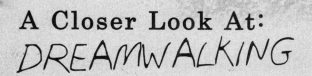

What are your deepest, darkest secrets? What about your worst fears?

Now imagine someone else learning those private thoughts and using them against you… in your own subconscious dreams. Dreams so vivid you can't differentiate them from reality. And even if you realize you're dreaming, you can't wake up because this other person, this *dreamwalker*, is controlling your dream.

Talk about a living nightmare!

Silene capensis, a.k.a. 'African dream root', has been used by shaman and medicine men for centuries. It's an oneirogen, which derives its name from the Greek *oneiros* meaning 'dream' and *gen* meaning 'to create', because it produces a dreamlike state of consciousness. Other oneirogens used for dreamwalking are *Calea zacatechichi*, a.k.a. the 'dream herb', and *Entada rheedii*, a.k.a. 'African dream herb'.

SAM: If you believe the legends, it's used for dreamwalking. I mean, entering another person's dreams… poking around in their heads.
DEAN: I take it we believe the legends.
SAM: When don't we?

'The right dosage of any of these plants (although the most potent is African dream root), prepared and ingested the right way, should allow you to dreamwalk. At first you can just look around other people's dreams, but then you can delve deeper and poke around in their memories, and then, if you take it regularly, and with enough practice, you can control anything. You can turn bad dreams good or turn good dreams into nightmares. A skilled dreamwalker can even kill people in their sleep…

"We always change the lore a little bit to make it suit our story," Cathryn Humphris observes. "There are cultures that believe in dreamwalking, but no one has ever proven that it exists."

Scientists have proven that oneirogens bring about more vivid and colorful dreams, as well as increasing the frequency of dreams, and improving the recall of dreams upon waking.

"Some people take this drug and go on a vision quest," Humphris reveals. "For days you're supposedly just purging the demons from inside you."

MYSTERY SPOT

Written by:
Jeremy Carver,
Emily McLaughlin

Directed by:
Kim Manners

Guest Cast: Katherine Horsman (Ms. Hasselback), David Abbott (Judge Myers), Derek Green (Ed), Denalda Williams (Doris), Dean Moen (Randy), Lloyd Berry (Mr. Pickett), Rob deLeeuw (Clem), Brock Johnson (Sid), Richard Speight Jr. (Trickster), Andrew McIlroy (P.J. Karpiak), Denalda Williams (Doris), Kasey Keiler (Kel)

A man disappears after visiting the Broward County Mystery Spot — a tourist destination "Where the Laws of Physics Have No Meaning". It's Tuesday, and while Sam and Dean search the site, Dean is shot and killed by the owner. Devastated, Sam suddenly wakes up in his motel room to find Dean alive and well... but they're reliving the same day. Sam tries to prevent Dean's death, but Dean gets hit by a car this time, and dies.

It's Tuesday, again and again, and each time, Dean dies again and again. He gets crushed by a falling desk, chokes on a sausage, slips in the shower, eats a "funny" taco, is electrocuted by his shaver, gets accidentally "axed" by Sam, and is mauled by a dog — despite Sam's efforts to keep him safe.

Sam eventually figures out it's the Trickster and confronts him. The Trickster says revenge for them trying to kill him is not his motive — he's actually trying to teach Sam that he cannot save Dean from going to Hell. Sam threatens him, and the Trickster severs the loop. It's finally Wednesday... but Dean gets shot by a mugger and dies. This time, there's no 'reset'.

Sam hunts the Trickster for months (while killing other monsters along the way), until Bobby tells him he has found a summoning ritual that needs a human sacrifice. Sam doesn't care, but when 'Bobby' insists Sam should kill him, Sam realizes it's the Trickster. Sam promises the Trickster that he and Dean won't pursue him, so the Trickster, claiming to be bored of the joke, returns him to the normal timeline, with Dean waking up alive on Wednesday. But the Trickster's parting words, "That's for me to know and you to find out," implies he's not through with the brothers yet...

DEAN: I'm tellin' you, Sam, this job is small fry. We should be spending our time huntin' down Bela.
SAM: Okay. Sure. Let's get right on that. Where is she again?
DEAN: Shut up.

"My mother wasn't real thrilled with this episode," remarks Jensen Ackles. "My dad, of course, thought it was hilarious, and I liked it. Maybe I'm just sick, but I was really attracted to the script. As I was reading it, I was like, 'That's going to be funny!'" Richard Speight Jr. had the same reaction. "I read that script and I was laughing out loud," he says.

DID YOU KNOW?

Filming the exact same day over and over again proved to be a challenge for director of photography Serge Ladouceur. "We'd done a lot of it in the sun and then suddenly we had to do one scene where it was overcast..."

"But the bottom line is that it's torturous for Sam," Ackles adds. "It's really heartbreaking."

"That was a hard episode for me to shoot," acknowledges Jared Padalecki. "I'm not a method actor, but you have to find the truth in that, see where the character would be, and put yourself in that mindset. It's like, 'I don't want to think about how I'd feel or how I'd react. Can't we just go back to arguing? I like to argue. Can't I just argue with him? Why do I have to watch him die over and over?' I really worked hard to put myself in the moment. It was funny — I kept laughing, because Jensen had to keep getting all this fake blood put over him, so he was getting sticky. But once they say, 'cameras ready', you have to get out of that laugh mode and get right back into depressing, watching your brother die mode... which is not a fun place to be for a week and a half.

"I got to enjoy it as an audience member when watching it later, and it was hilarious. My favorite was when we were fighting over the axe and you just kind of hear it and see the blood splatter. That was a really clever way to do it, and it was fun because I kill Dean." Writer Emily McLaughlin agrees. "My favorite is when Dean gets the axe. That one makes me laugh the hardest. Figuring out all of Dean's deaths was hysterical.

"The *Groundhog Day*-type cycle came first, the idea to 'fake' kill Dean came soon after, and the idea to do another Trickster episode brought all the pieces together. I am extremely happy with the way it turned out, and to see my name on such a classy episode of *Supernatural* is unreal," McLaughlin shares.

Above
Dean shows Sam what he got from the girl he kept bumping into.

DID YOU KNOW?

On the placemats in the diner there's an image of a ground-hog, and it's a children's coloring contest to win a bicycle. Everyone in the *Supernatural* art department colored their own groundhog, and they have a collage of them on the wall.

SAM: You don't remember any of this?
DEAN: Remember what?
SAM: This. Today. Like it's happened before?
DEAN: You mean like déjà vu?
SAM: No, I mean like... like it's *really* happened before.
DEAN: Yeah. *Like...* déjà vu.
SAM: No. Forget about déjà vu. I'm asking you if it feels like we're living yesterday all over again?
DEAN: Okay... how is that not dé—
SAM: Don't say it! Just don't.

Padalecki and Ackles had a different kind of "unreal" experience on the set of 'Mystery Spot' when the crew pranked them. "Jared and Jensen are both from Texas, and I'm from Green Bay [Wisconsin]," notes production designer Jerry Wanek. "There was a big [Cowboys versus Packers] football game, so while they were shooting, I put Packers memorabilia all over their trailers, including life-sized Brett Favre posters. I even got the caterer in on it and had him make Wisconsin bratwurst for lunch. The boys were shooting at this auto place. They were inside, and I had the AD ask them some stupid questions just to distract them. When Kim Manners yelled 'Action', everybody on the crew put on a Brett Favre mask and a Packers helmet, so as Jared and Jensen came out the door, they saw seventy-five Brett Favres staring at them! The boys have a great sense of humor, so they just went along with it and had fun. That night I watched the game in Jensen's trailer and Dallas killed Green Bay, so they got their revenge."

Speight Jr. was invited to watch the game in Ackles' trailer, too. "I was like, 'That's great, I don't have to go sit in my hotel by myself,'" he recalls. "Their trailers are side by side, and I couldn't remember who was airing the game, so I go to Jared's trailer and knock. I hear some sort of noise — what I think is a 'Come in!' — so I open the door and take two steps in... and instead of seeing Jared and Jensen, I see two flipping giant dogs. I don't know what breed, but clearly they could bite my face off. I look at them and they look at me and then they perk up. I soil myself and run like a bat out of hell, closing the door right as they leap off the couch toward me. So in the boys' attempt to welcome me into the circle and watch the football game, I almost got killed by breaking and entering into Jared's trailer. I was so embarrassed! I've never told Jared this story, so it'll be news to him."

"'Mystery Spot' was kind of comical for us," points out visual effects coordinator Ivan Hayden. "As soon as it gets comical, it allows a bit of forgiveness, which lets us have a lot more fun. We get to take things a little bit further, make it a little bit sillier, and no one's going to go, 'That doesn't look real,' because of the tone of the episode. For example, when Dean gets electrocuted, you actually see his skeleton. We killed ourselves laughing."

"I thought 'Mystery Spot' worked on all levels," proclaims executive producer Kim Manners, "and that's the mark of a great hour of television. It was entertaining, funny, scary, emotional... it had every element." ✧

MUSIC

'Heat of the Moment' by Asia
'Back In Time' by Huey Lewis & The News

Below

Sam is horrified to find Dean dead on Wednesday.

A Closer Look At:

MYSTERY SPOTS

There are spots around the world where wormholes (shortcuts through space and time) open up and swallow people... cars... boats... planes. Scary, but true.

Everyone's heard of the Bermuda Triangle, and there are so many stories surrounding that region of the Atlantic Ocean (also known as the Devil's Triangle) that it'd take a whole book, maybe even a whole library, to do this amazing phenomenon justice. Suffice it to say that it is known for being the sight of frequent unexplained disappearances of ships and aircraft, the most famous being the USS *Cyclops*, which went missing in March 1918. An entire Proteus-class collier, along with its 306 crew and passengers, vanished without a trace. The popular belief is that the Bermuda Triangle has a fluctuating wormhole of extraterrestrial origins (possibly even generated by a powerful teleportation device), while others believe that within the Bermuda Triangle the laws of earthly physics do not apply. But recent investigations by hunters have uncovered signs that the wormhole is supernatural in origin.

P.J. KARPIAK: Strange happens here all the time. It's a Mystery Spot!
SAM: What exactly does that mean?
P.J. KARPIAK: Well, um...it's where the laws of physics have no meaning.
SAM: Okay. Like *how*?
P.J. KARPIAK: Take the tour.

On the opposite side of the world, south of Japan, is the Pacific Ocean's version of the Bermuda Triangle, known to the area's fishermen as the Dragon's Triangle. The region is also called the Devil's Sea, and the number of ships and aircraft that have gone missing there is even greater than in the Bermuda Triangle. There have also been numerous sightings of ghost ships and UFOs. The Dragon's Triangle is most likely where beloved American aviator Amelia Earhart left our world.

On a smaller (but no less weird) scale is the Michigan Triangle. Located over central Lake Michigan, this mysterious spot is riddled with strange disappearances, time fluctuations, sightings of cryptozoological and supernatural creatures, and other unusual activity.

Some believe these mystery spots are portals to the fabled city of Atlantis, which resides in the 'Hollow Earth' at the center of our planet. Ultimately, no one knows for sure if these wormholes go to other dimensions, other eras, alien worlds, Atlantis, or Hell... because if anyone's made a round trip, they're not talking.

Another common type of mystery spot (visited by millions of people) is the non-wormhole type, often just called the Mystery Spot. It's theorized that extraterrestrials buried unearthly metals or spacecraft beneath them, which messes with earthly physics. But most hunters suspect that these locations are supernatural hotspots. Sadly, most of the time, places like the Broward County Mystery Spot — "where the laws of physics have no meaning" — are just hoaxes. They're tourist traps that employ optical illusions and forced perceptions. Rooms are built at unusual angles, using the skewed atmosphere inside the mystery spots to cause misconceptions of the height and orientation of objects, and dressed with furniture nailed to the ceiling, and so forth.

"It's amazing, almost every state has one of these," Jerry Wanek confirms. "They were much more popular in the sixties and seventies, when people were just starting to spend a lot of time in their cars, taking the freeways to these little hamlets and stuff. They're all basically optical illusions, but the amount of time spent engineering these illusions is pretty impressive and it's amazing how they pulled that stuff off. We found enough research from all these different mystery spots that we just took their concept and extrapolated it, and put it into our *Supernatural* environment."

SAM: Well, sometimes these places are legit.
DEAN: Alright. So if it is legit — and that's a big-ass "if" — what's the lore?
SAM: The lore's pretty friggin' nuts, actually. They say in these places, the magnetic fields are so strong that they can bend space-time. Sending victims... no one knows where.

Note, however, that not all of these mystery spots are manufactured. The hoaxes are merely clever attempts to mimic *real* mystery spots. One way to know you're in a real mystery spot is if your GPS unit goes haywire and tries to tell you that you're somewhere you're definitely not. I suggest you take a road trip and check them all out to discover for yourself which ones are the real deal. But don't bring your pets — cats and dogs are known to freak out from the unusual energies in mystery spots.

Here's a far from exhaustive list to get you started: Buena Park, California; Calico Ghost Town Mystery Shack, California; Confusion Hill at Idlewild Park, Pennsylvania; Cosmos of the Black Hills, South Dakota; Gravity House, California; Knott's Berry Farm, California; Marblehead Mystery Hill, Ohio; Mystery Hill, Michigan; Mystery Shack, North Carolina; Oregon Vortex, Oregon; Santa Cruz Mystery Spot, California; St. Ignace Mystery Spot, Michigan; Spook Hill, Florida; and Wonder Spot, Wisconsin. There's even one called the Winchester Mystery House in San Jose, California.

Have fun, but don't step into any wormholes…

MIS
THE FAMILY AND
ARE DESPERATELY ASK
IN LOCATING HIM. M

DEXTER HA
Description:
Height:
Weight: 5'11"
Complexion: 170 lbs
fai

JUS IN BELLO

Written by: Sera Gamble

Directed by: Phil Sgriccia

Guest Cast: Aimee Garcia (Nancy Fitzgerald), Peter DeLuise (Steven Groves), Charles Malik Whitfield (Victor Henriksen), Val Cole (News Reporter), Rachel Pattee (Lilith), Kurt Evans (Agent Reidy), Ron Robinson (Cop), Tyler McClendon (Deputy Phil Amici), Stoney Westmoreland (Sheriff Dodd)

Sam and Dean track Bela to Monument, Colorado, and break into her motel room. There's no Colt, but there *is* a trap — cops bust down the door, followed by Agent Henriksen. While the brothers are locked inside a cell at the local sheriff's office, a demon-possessed FBI agent shoots Dean in the shoulder before Sam casts the demon out. Meanwhile, other demons kill some of the local law enforcement, and a possessed Henriksen shoots the sheriff. Sam and Dean manage to exorcise his demon, and the FBI agent admits he was wrong and releases them.

Realizing they are being besieged by demons, the brothers take command and set up defenses throughout the building. Temporarily safe, they distribute protection amulets and reveal the ones they have tattooed on their chests.

Ruby appears and informs them that Lilith, the demon who would be queen, has sent thirty demons after them. She tries to convince Sam to use a spell that will vaporize every demon within a one-mile radius — including herself — but Dean refuses, as it means sacrificing a virgin, though they have a volunteer, Nancy. He convinces Sam that they should just fight. Disappointed, Ruby leaves.

The demons storm in and a huge brawl ensues. Outside, Nancy and a deputy reseal all the doors with salt. One demon escapes, but the rest are exorcised by a prerecorded exorcism played over the loudspeakers. Afterward, Henriksen tells FBI headquarters that the Winchesters died in the siege.

Shortly after the boys leave, Lilith arrives in the form of a little girl and kills everyone — including Henriksen and Nancy — with a wall of deadly white energy. Ruby then tells Sam and Dean that all those deaths are on them.

HENRIKSEN: Five minutes ago I was fine. And then...
DEAN: Let me guess. Nasty black smoke jammed itself down your throat?
SAM: You were possessed.
HENRIKSEN: "Possessed" like... *possessed?*
SAM: That's what it feels like. Now you know.
DEAN: I owe you the biggest I-told-you-so ever.

While you'd think it'd be a good idea for everyone to get a tattoo that protects them from demon possessions, the tattoos that Jared Padalecki and Jensen Ackles sport in 'Jus in Bello' were indeed just special effects makeup. "I don't have any ink," Ackles reveals. "I'm not against it. I've always said that if something really inspired me,

DID YOU KNOW?

Supervising sound editor Michael E. Lawshe and his team were nominated for an Emmy in the category Outstanding Sound Editing for a Series for this episode, but lost the award to... *themselves!* They won the Emmy for the *Smallville* episode 'Bizarro'.

then I wouldn't necessarily talk myself out of it. But so far I just haven't seen anything that I want to have permanently attached to my skin. I think it'd be kind of cool, actually, to see a fan with the amulet tattoo. I mean, you look at it, it's actually a pretty cool tattoo. People would be like, 'Wow, what is that?' If it means something to somebody, then why not?"

"I actually don't think I could ever get a tattoo," says Lauren Cohan, "because I think about one and decide on it and I pretend I have it for a month, and I'm already sick of it." Director Phil Sgriccia adds, "I'm not going to go do it, but to each his own."

"Phil Sgriccia was the director of pretty much all the episodes I've done," points out Charles Malik Whitfield. "What a genius mind he has. I was working with [producer/director] Jesse Bochco on this new show for TNT, *Raising the Bar*, and I said, 'Phil, I was so impressed with Jesse, he set up these shots that were so specific and he's one hell of a director.' I don't know why I said that to him! And Phil said, 'Really? That's great.' We worked an eighteen-hour day that day, and I swear he created the most ingenious shots. It was great for me because he did some amazing stuff, but that was one tiring day. I was like, 'Phil, I didn't tell you about Jesse so you'd one-up him.' But he totally one-upped him! Phil's the best director I've worked with, *ever.*"

Of the *Supernatural* episodes Whitfield's been in, 'Jus in Bello' is his favorite. "I liked teaming up with the guys because I got to play with guns and go through my whole stuntman action mode. That was fun."

Above

Old enemies become new allies.

"There was some tough stuff to do in there — fights in tight spaces, people putting fists through walls, people swinging from doorframes. It was nuts," exclaims stunt coordinator Lou Bollo. "One of the toughest was the demon who came running in, dove over the counter, and was shot in mid-air. He's an ex-NFL player. It's just unbelievable watching him fly over that and do it perfectly." Padalecki's stunt double, Michael Carpenter, was on the receiving end of that flying demon. "I remember blasting off a shotgun at Ronny Robinson. You see a guy that size barreling down on you, you want to hope that shotgun goes off. That was fun."

Despite having a talented double, Padalecki chooses to do his own stunts whenever possible. "When he gets thrown against stuff, we'll pad him up and sometimes we'll soften certain walls for him," says Bollo, "but his plan over all these years is to see if he can break the set. He really works at it. He's a big boy, and he's really strong. And in that particular set, he looked at this one wall he was supposed to get thrown against, looked up at the top, where the walls are built into the ceiling pieces, and said, 'I can break this.' So he goes back and flies into that wall... and he literally moved the set. It was unreal."

Sgriccia found working on parts of the episode pretty unreal at times, too. "Lots of

gunfire, lots of rock salt flying. We had thirty demons in the room at one time. It was challenging, because I had to keep it fresh and keep it moving. The extras that we got were really into it. Sometimes that's the hardest part, to not have any words but you have to act a certain way. A few of them had black contact lenses in. It was challenging, and it was in a small space of the police station that we built. That was one of the biggest sets that we'd built."

HENRIKSEN: So. Turns out demons are real.
DEAN: FYI, ghosts are real, too. So are werewolves, vampires, changelings, evil clowns that eat people...
HENRIKSEN: Okay then.
DEAN: If it makes you feel any better, Bigfoot's a hoax.
HENRIKSEN: It doesn't.

"I think anybody watching that thought we were at a real police precinct," asserts production designer Jerry Wanek. "It was very cool because we got to build this complete police precinct. It gave us a chance to do something in seventies architecture, which was fun."

"It was sort of a trade-off," notes producer Sera Gamble. "We'll do it all in one location, but then we'll get more demons into that location. We had to deliver a demon war at some point of the season, and we thought 'Jus in Bello' might end up being the season finale because it was the last episode before the strike. I think Phil did an amazing job directing it." ✍

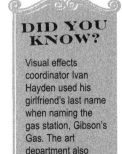

DID YOU KNOW?

Visual effects coordinator Ivan Hayden used his girlfriend's last name when naming the gas station, Gibson's Gas. The art department also used a photo of Phil Sgriccia's daughter for one of the wanted posters.

GHOSTFACERS

Written by:
Ben Edlund

Directed by:
Phil Sgriccia

Guest Cast: Travis Wester (Harry Spangler), Dustin Milligan (Alan J. Corbett), A.J. Buckley (Ed Zeddmore), John DeSantis (Freeman Daggett), Austin Basis (Kenny Spruce), Tony Morelli (Staggering Man), Brittany Ishibashi (Maggie Zeddmore), Dave Hospes (Travelling Salesman)

The Hellhounds (from 'Hell House') are back. Only now they're the Ghostfacers! Ed Zeddmore and Harry Spangler have recruited three teammates — Spruce, the camera guy; Corbett, the intern (who has romantic feelings for Ed); and Maggie, Ed's adopted sister — and are producing their own reality show about their exploits confronting ghosts. Their latest attempt at notoriety brings them to the Morton House, which every four years becomes the most haunted place in America thanks to Freeman Daggett, "The Leap Year Ghost". No one's ever stayed through the night, but they plan to be the first... and get it all on video.

Everything's running smoothly until those amateur hunters who messed everything up in Texas barge in uninvited. The pair of chisel-chests, Sam and Dean, try to convince the Ghostfacers to leave, but the clock strikes midnight and all the exits are sealed supernaturally. Some ghosts appear, caught in death echoes, replaying their deaths in a loop. They seem harmless enough, but something isn't right — one of them is repeatedly run over by a train, yet there are no tracks nearby.

First Corbett, then Sam is kidnapped by the Leap Year Ghost, and Dean and the Ghostfacers begin a frantic search. The heightened emotions of the situation bring out Harry and Maggie's feelings for each other, which incenses Ed. But they're soon distracted by another death echo, this time of their friend Corbett being killed by Daggett somewhere in the house. Dean and Spruce find Sam in a bomb shelter beneath the house, but Daggett is too strong for the three of them... and Spruce is about to join Corbett. Ed tells Corbett how much he means to him and the team, and his love pulls Corbett from his death echo. Corbett's spirit is ready to move on... and he takes Daggett with him!

Excited with their footage, the Ghostfacers show their pilot to Sam and Dean, who disparage them for exploiting Corbett's death. To add injury to insult, the Facer Haters leave behind a large electromagnet that erases all of the Ghostfacers' hard drives.

MAGGIE: Ed has been obsessed with the supernatural since we were kids, y'know? Then, he meets Harry at computer camp and... love at first geek.

"'Ghostfacers' was the most fun I had in season three," notes co-executive producer Ben Edlund, "and I think it came out well." Creator Eric Kripke agrees. "I loved it

from the moment Ben first came up with it. He comes into the room and says, 'Hey, do you remember those two characters, Ed and Harry from season one, the Hellhounds? Well, I think they have their own reality show, and I think they're filming an episode of their reality show on video and Sam and Dean stumble into their reality show. Their show is called *Ghostfacers* and here's the theme song, I wrote it over the weekend.' So he sang us the theme song and asked, 'What do you think?' We were like, 'You had us at the theme song.'"

"That was a fantastic episode because I got to sing on the theme song from *Ghostfacers*," enthuses composer Chris Lennertz. "Ben Edlund came over to the studio and I played all the guitars and we made the silliest theme song we could come up with. We both screamed into the microphone and I thought it was super funny."

"That was a really fun part," states A.J. Buckley. Brittany Ishibashi elaborates. "All of us got to go into the studio and record like rock stars, which was a lot of fun. We talked about doing a mock tribute to the MTV show *Making the Band*, and do some Ghostfacers garage band stuff with Maggie on keys, Harry on lead guitar, and Ed on bass. But I think I'll stick with acting."

"One of the things I did in 'Ghostfacers' was I treated it like a reality show," notes Lennertz, "so I scored it with really cheesy synthesizers and tried to make it sound like something they would do. I made it sound lame on purpose. We don't usually get

Above

Ghostfacers Harry (Travis Wester) and Ed (A.J. Buckley) pitch their reality show.

Above

Dean is surprised that the Ghostfacers actually caught a ghost on video.

MUSIC

'We're an American Band' by Grand Funk Railroad

'Hocus Pocus' by Focus

'It's My Party' by Leslie Gore

asked to do that."

Actors don't normally get asked to carry their own cameras and lights, either. "It's definitely as far removed from our normal work habits as possible," Jensen Ackles reflects. "There's essentially no camera crews, no sound crews, no grips... I mean, they were all there, but none of them were on set, which was just strange. Normally, you have to hit your mark, you have to find your light, you have to find your camera, you can't be blocking people. There's so much to think about aside from the performance that it's almost got to be second nature... so to take all that away and just allow the performance was pretty liberating." Padalecki concurs. "You got to just exist in this supernatural realm. You got to be in the moment, and we were allowed to improvise, too."

"We laughed from the start of the day to the end," admits Sgriccia. "The actors playing the Ghostfacers were great improv actors. We did a whole raft of stuff that wasn't scripted. Ben gave me a bunch of extra questions to ask, like, 'What makes you scared?' 'What do you think of Sam and Dean?' Everybody reads the script, so I like to throw in monkey wrenches to get real reactions on stuff. Like, I threw in the whole rat thing. I put the rat on the floor and I didn't tell Travis it was going to be there."

Travis Weston enjoyed the surprises Sgriccia threw his way. "We just played with it," he says. "When we did the confessionals, Harry had that whole thing where he's like, 'I don't like rats.'"

"It was so funny because it was such a genuine reaction," Ishibashi declares. "Travis really freaked out. It was one of those things that kept the energy on the set

very light and fun."

Buckley confirms, "We just could not stop laughing, and once Jared starts laughing, he physically can't stop laughing. Plus, Jared's a giant, so he laughs with a giant laugh and the room shakes. Sometimes he'd be laughing so hard he'd fall and lay on the ground and laugh. There was just a lot of great banter between us all."

DEAN: There's some salt in my duffel. Make a circle and get inside.
ED: Inside your duffel bag?
DEAN: In the salt, you idiots!

Ishibashi shares a fond memory. "When we're storming the Morton House, they had this beautiful set up with all this fog coming in, and we were running over this rickety bridge over a stream and running through all this mud, and at one point Harry slips and falls. He's covered in mud and we're running through all this stuff, and we've got flashlights and little packs, and at one point we cut and stopped and looked at each other and we were like, 'These are the games you'd play when you were seven with your neighbors in your backyard. It's like they built this life-size haunted house for us to play in and we're getting paid for it!' All of us involved, including Phil, felt like big kids during this shoot, which was really cool."

LONG-DISTANCE CALL

Written by: Jeremy Carver

Directed by: Robert Singer

Guest Cast: Ingrid Torrance (Margaret Waters), Eric Breker (Mike Stubbs), Thomas Michael Dobie (Ed), Dawson Dunbar (Simon Greenfield), John Shaw (Ben Waters), David Neale (Mark Greenfield), Anna Mae Routledge (Museum Guide), Anjul Nigam (Stewie Myers), Tom O'Brien (Clark Adams/Crocotta), Cherilyn Wilson (Lanie Greenfield)

When Bobby tips Dean off to a malevolent spirit in Milan, Ohio, the brothers butt heads because Sam feels they should focus on breaking Dean's deal. Dean says they've exhausted all their resources, but Sam argues they should ask Ruby for help. Dean reveals that Ruby admitted she couldn't help him, so they set off for Ohio, where the dead are phoning their loved ones.

Then Dean is stunned when their dad calls.

They're led to the Edison Museum, where they scan Thomas Edison's "Spirit Phone" with their EMF meter, but the needle doesn't even waver. They wonder if the phone could be acting like a radio tower, broadcasting the dead all over town. Then John phones back, saying the demon who holds Dean's contract is in Milan, and giving Dean an exorcism that'll kill it. Sam is skeptical and argues that something else is going on, so he goes to see a girl whose dead mother has been calling her, while Dean takes off to find the demon.

Sam deduces that they're dealing with a crocotta, a supernatural creature that mimics human voices and gets victims to kill themselves so he can swallow their departing souls. But when Sam calls Dean to warn him, the crocotta pretends to be Dean and lures Sam into a trap. Dean comes close to killing an innocent man, but realizes he's made a horrible mistake when holy water and a devil's trap have no effect. Sam is nearly killed by the crocotta, but gets the upper hand and eliminates the beast.

Dean apologizes for fighting with Sam and admits that he's really scared about going to Hell.

DEAN: What if it really is dad? What happens if he calls back?
SAM: What do you mean?
DEAN: What do I say?
SAM: Hello?

"If you call Eric Kripke, Bob Singer, or the writers up and ask them what a crocotta is, they can tell you what it had for breakfast yesterday morning!" proclaims visual effects supervisor Ivan Hayden. "They research this stuff to the nth degree. We use that information, and there are collaborations between [the visual effects department] and the art department. But most of the times, in instances like the

crocotta, with its growing jaw, it really comes down to what we can do in the time, budget, and parameters of our show."

Sometimes the budget doesn't allow for renting set pieces, such as Edison's real Spirit Phone. "Apparently he built one," set decorator George Neuman relates. "Supposedly, you can actually contact the dead. It was owned by a museum in San Diego, but a collector bought it off eBay for $5,000. So we contacted this guy about possibly renting it, but it was going to cost too much to bring it in. Instead, we had to go down to a radio museum in Bellingham, Washington, that had something similar. So Jerry Wanek and I drove down there — and I almost got arrested!

"What happened was Jerry's American and he's got a Nexus pass, so he can go across the border quickly, but only Jerry's allowed to cross using the pass. Previously he'd done it where he'd drop a passenger off at the border and they'd walk in and go through customs there. So he dropped me off and drove through... but I went inside and they're like, 'He did what? You're not allowed to do that!'" Neuman elaborates. "Apparently they don't do that anymore at this particular border crossing. To make matters worse, there was a code something-or-other going on at the time — fifteen to twenty officers were out there with their guns drawn, pulling a guy out of his car. It was heightened security and they were on edge, but in the end, they allowed me through."

If it's not budgets or border patrols causing issues, then it's scheduling. For the scene in the phone company's basement, location manager Russ Hamilton found the

Above

Sam and Dean just need to look at their motel room's bedspreads to remember they're in Ohio.

perfect place, "but it didn't work for the schedule, so we built that piece here. We're often driven by the schedule, because the page count justifies going out to location. In this case, that really cool part was shot here."

The basement scenes were especially cool thanks to the memorable performance of Anjul Nigam. "The guy who played Stewie was a great actor," exclaims writer Jeremy Carver. "When I wrote Stewie, I pictured him as a big sloppy guy, but Anjul Nigam played him differently and better than I could've imagined."

DEAN: Wow, man, a couple of civvies are freaked out by some ghosts. Newsflash, Sam — people are *supposed* to be freaked out by ghosts!

"He was supposed to be a geeky guy who doesn't get out much, but still thinks he's cool," explains key hair stylist Jeannie Chow. "So we gave him really greasy hair." Costume designer Diane Widas approached the character's look the same way. "We were trying to make him that geeky kind of guy that everybody knows, who tries to have a bit of style, but it's not quite working 'cause he's got too many layers and his clothes are a bit too small on him and whatever. We really had fun with him because he played along with it and wanted to push the envelope, too."

The art department also enhanced Stewie's personality, as graphic designer Lee Anne Elaschuk relates. "Stewie has an 'Employees of the Month' poster, with all the employees who have won some sort of award on it. [Graphic designer] Mary Ann Liu did this hilarious poster of all the people who work there, but Stewie is the type of guy who'd graffiti the images, so we passed the poster around the art department and everyone put graffiti on someone else. It turned out to be very funny. That's what someone like that would do — he'd be that bad-attitude kind of guy who works in the basement. He would have it in for the employees who have it better than him."

But at least he wouldn't have it in for them the way Mike Stubbs had it in for Dean, who he thought had murdered his daughter. According to stunt coordinator Lou Bollo, Stubbs fought the way "you or I would if pushed to the wall. We're not martial artists, we don't get in bar fights or anything. It's how you would behave with rage," he explains. "It's just striking brutally at anything you can, any way you can, just trying to destroy what's in front of you."

Editor Tom McQuade enjoyed the fighting style in that scene. "Very rarely do you see a repeat of style on this show," he points out. "I can't say enough about how each episode is different. That's because the stories don't do that, each director brings something different, and I think we editors all turn out different looking episodes. I assume people like that." ✡

TIME IS ON MY SIDE

Written by:
Sera Gamble

Directed by:
Charles Beeson

Guest Cast: Nathaniel Marten (Jogger), Roan Curtis (Schoolgirl Demon), Tiera Skovbye (Young Bela), Kaleena Kiff (Young Woman), Craig Veroni (Thomas), Marilyn Norry (Nurse), Kavan Smith (Jules), Terence Kelly (Coroner), Adrian Holmes (Demon), Steven Williams (Rufus Turner), Peter Birkenhead (Victim), Billy Drago (Doc Benton)

A rash of organ thefts in Erie, Pennsylvania, puts the Winchester brothers on the trail of Doc Benton, a doctor who abandoned his medical practice in 1816 and succeeded in finding the key to eternal life through alchemy, though he needs to replace body parts whenever they wear out or get damaged. In order to save Dean from going to Hell, Sam intends to obtain the formula, but Dean argues that becoming immortal is cheating.

Dean decides that retrieving the Colt and killing the demon who holds his contract is still his best option. He seeks out Bobby's friend, hunter Steven Williams, and learns that Bela killed her parents when she was fourteen. Dean confronts her, but the Colt is long gone, and he can't bring himself to shoot her in cold blood.

Meanwhile, Sam rescues a woman from Doc Benton, steals the formula, and runs the doctor over. But then Benton chloroforms Sam and straps him to his operating table. Dean rushes in before Sam loses an eyeball and stabs the doctor with a chloroform-dipped knife. They bury him alive, chained in an old refrigerator, and Dean declares that becoming like that monster would be worse than going to Hell.

Bela shows up at the brothers' motel room and shoots blow-up dolls she thinks are them. Dean calls Bela and guesses the truth: she's running from hellhounds because she failed to kill Sam for Lilith, the demon she sold her soul to when she wanted her abusive father killed. Before the hellhounds drag her away, she reveals that Lilith holds Dean's contract, and Lillith is the demon leader gunning for Sam.

CORONER: Can I see your badges?
SAM: Of course, sure—
CORONER: Fine, so, you're cops. And morons.
DEAN: Excuse me? No. No — we're *very* smart.

"Right from the opening we've got someone dropping their guts on the floor, so I kept saying, 'Is anyone going to come arrest me after this has been aired?'" jokes director Charles Beeson. "Of course, when you're doing that, you're sort of outside the experience of it. You say, 'Just hold the guts like that, then I'll give you a shout, and then just drop all your guts on the floor.' You have your composure as if you're saying, 'I need you to park by the red car there.' So it's all kind of matter of fact, but every now and again you think, 'What are we doing here?' Lifting out beating hearts is extreme, particularly when they look that good. It's amazing what does get on the air now."

Above
Doc Benton attempts
to perform open heart
surgery on Sam.

"I'm really surprised pulling that heart out got past standards and practices," comments producer Todd Aronauer. "It made me squirm in my seat when you see the rusty melonballer with jagged edges pressing against Sam's eye. It certainly is a very graphic episode." Beeson points out that "You don't want the audience turning away from the screen, but it's about telling the story and telling it in the right way to make it work."

What really makes those types of things work is the quality of the effects. "All the guys who do the special effects and visual effects and prosthetics and stuff like that, they're just brilliant," Beeson proclaims, "and usually very ambitious. You go in there and say what you think is probably impossible, and they somehow make it work. For Doc Benton's face, you could stand an inch away from that and it held up. Absolutely amazing." Jensen Ackles agrees. "The makeup that our special effects makeup department did on Billy Drago was just unbelievable. It just looked so real."

Of course, some things were very real, like the maggots on Kaleena Kiff's arm. "We had her arm layered up in prosthetics… but then covered in maggots," says Toby Lindala, head of special effects makeup. "A maggot wrangler would count them every day and make sure that no maggots were harmed. They even had their own little trailer… We used rice for some of the running through the fields stuff so that she's not dropping the actual maggots."

Above

Bela returns to her hotel room... to find Dean waiting for her.

"I had no idea it would be that disgusting," states Kiff. "I mean, really wrong; the foul, fishy smell, the tickle as they squirmed down my arm, the coldness of their little bodies. In the dailies, I'm writhing on the table, strapped down and moaning until they call action, then it was almost an out of body experience how I just went completely still. Crazy mind over matter." Of course, Kiff wasn't disgusted by being carried through the woods by Jared Padalecki. "Though Jared's not very charming or handsome, it proved useful to have such a large fellow carry me through the woods, as it was so cold and his big arms certainly kept me warm."

Kiff has a history in television, where she's probably best known for playing Kelley Cleaver on *Still the Beaver*, but her job on *Supernatural* is behind the camera as assistant to executive producer Kim Manners, so she wasn't expecting to be asked to play the Young Woman victim. "Honestly, I think it was an elaborate hazing process to welcome me into the *Supernatural* family," she insists. "I'd only been working on the show for about two weeks before my scenes shot, so I kept playing along, thinking they were kidding. Not until my arm was elbow deep in a vat of plaster did I finally realize they were serious!"

CORONER: Didn't you read my report?
DEAN: Of course we did. Oh, it was riveting, a real page-turner. Just delightful.
CORONER: You done?
DEAN: I think so.
CORONER: Please go away.

Beeson was very serious about Bela's backstory. "I was keen to make her end resonate," he says. "I tried to make her past as painful as possible, so that you got more of a sense of where she'd come from, to understand her more before the hellhounds ripped her up."

"I cut the episode that wrapped up Bela and I thought that was really clever what happened to her," opines editor Tom McQuade. "It pushed the story forward *and* wrapped up her character. I liked that a lot."

Jensen Ackles says he "was surprised they killed her off, but not surprised they wrote her off, which I don't think is any fault of Lauren Cohan's whatsoever. She's a wonderful person and a great actress. I just don't think the character was written in a way that tied her strongly enough to the boys."

"We made a valiant attempt," producer Sera Gamble asserts, "but she wasn't associated closely enough with the mythology of the season. We told the super short version of her story in the last couple of episodes, and that's that for her. The hellhounds came to take her away…"

That's that? Bela's not going to meet up with Dean in Hell? "Hell is a really, really big place," states Gamble, "so no." 〆

Below

Dean shows Bela how handy he is with guns.

A Closer Look At:
CROCOTTA

The crocotta are solitary creatures, hiding alone in the woods for days, weeks, or even months. They whisper to people to draw them into the dark woods at night. They are skilled at mimicking human voices, and can easily trick people into believing a loved one is calling them. Usually they pretend to be a human in danger, making the unwary victim rush to "save" them — but there's no saving you once a crocotta has you in its grasp and is devouring your soul.

Crocotta were once large hyena-like beasts, originating from India and Ethiopia, but they have evolved to the point where they can shapeshift into human form, changing color and gender at will. You won't know you're dealing with a crocotta until just before you die, when they unhinge their jaws and their spiked teeth spring forth as they open wide to swallow your soul.

Not much else is known about these clever creatures, other than that they tend to live in filth, so be wary of any seemingly clean locale that has an unusual number of flies, because chances are there's a crocotta hiding behind an illusion of human normalcy.

SAM: It's a crocotta.
DEAN: Is that a sandwich?
SAM: Some kind of scavenger. Mimics loved ones. Whispers, "Come to me," then lures you into the dark and swallows your soul—

"There's not a lot of lore about the crocotta," admits Jeremy Carver. "Truth be told, I'm not sure that Eric Kripke wasn't a little bit concerned that there wasn't enough lore about the crocotta. He kept saying to me, 'Maybe we can find another monster. Maybe we can find another monster.' Then he'd say, 'We just need a monster who can do this, this, and this...' And the only monster I could find was the crocotta! Maybe it's a little bit obscure, but it fit the bill in this case.

"The only time the lore was bent was giving the crocotta the ability to actually control the phone lines in the manner that he did. We took the mimicking and extrapolated. For *Supernatural*, the monsters are adapted to use their skills in a modern age."

Some legends say that when you place the striped eyeball of a slain crocotta under your tongue, it'll give you clairvoyant powers. Because of this, their eyes fetch a pretty penny — if you have a good broker like Bela — so the crocotta are being hunted into extinction.

A Closer Look At:
CHEATING DEATH

DEAN: Zombie with skills? 'Dr. Quinn, Medicine Zombie'?
SAM: Maybe we're on the wrong track, Dean — looking for hacked-up corpses.
DEAN: Then what should we be looking for?
SAM: Survivors. This isn't zombie lunch. It's organ theft.

Do you want to live forever?

Of course! Right? What have you got to lose? Well, try your humanity for one thing. Just look at Doc Benton.

Doc Benton was a real-life doctor that lived in New Hampshire. A brilliant alchemist, he was obsessed with learning how to live forever. In 1816 he abandoned his practice and disappeared into the woods — then people started turning up dead, missing organs and all kinds of body parts. Whatever he did to himself worked, because nearly two hundred years later, he's still seen roaming the area.

Then there's Frankenstein's Monster, perhaps the most famous attempt at cheating death, although Dr. Frankenstein chickened out of trying his experiments on himself. Now, I know what you're thinking — Frankenstein's Monster is fictional, right? Sorta. What most people don't realize is that author Mary Shelley was inspired by a true story she'd heard when visiting the *real* Castle Frankenstein, about a notorious alchemist, Konrad Dippel. He had performed gruesome experiments with human bodies, attempting to transfer the soul of one cadaver into another, and been driven out of town by an angry mob.

And let's not forget the urban legend about people waking up in bathtubs filled with ice to find their kidneys or other organs missing. With people like Dippel and Benton out there, you can never be too careful…

Unless you're one of the lucky few who know the location of one of the world's Fountains of Youth, the only way to cheat death is to steal body parts and make yourself look like a grotesque human jigsaw puzzle. So, I'll ask you again: Do you want to live forever?

"No effing way!" Lauren Cohan responds without hesitation. "The older you get, the more peaceful you feel about everything. I look forward to getting old and dying one day."

"No, absolutely not," Jensen Ackles proclaims. "When you live forever, you have to watch all your loved ones around you die. I wouldn't want to have to deal with that."

"Definitely not," Eric Kripke concurs. "It sounds terrible — all your loved ones die and you're left alone to travel through eternity by yourself. Seems like torture. I can't think of anything worse."

NO REST FOR THE WICKED: IN DEPTH

Written by: Eric Kripke

Directed by: Kim Manners

Guest Cast: George Coe (Pat 'Grandpa' Fremont), Sierra McCormick (Zoey Fremont/Lilith), Jonathan Potts (Jimmy Fremont), Anna Galvin (Barbara Fremont), Brad Loree (Patrolman), Peter Hanlon (Tom Weprin), Vince Murdocco (Mailman)

The hellhounds have come to tear Dean's soul from his body! Fortunately, it's just a nightmare, and Dean wakes in a cold sweat rather than in burning hot Hellfire. But he only has thirty hours to go before his soul is forfeit. With Bobby's help, Sam and Dean learn that Lilith is in New Harmony, Indiana, on "vacation". Sam wants to summon Ruby so they can use her demon-killing knife on Lilith, but Dean refuses, saying, "We're not going to make the same mistake all over again."

With time running out, Sam ignores Dean and summons Ruby. She claims she didn't tell them about Lilith holding Dean's contract because she figured they'd have attacked unprepared and gotten their skins peeled from their bodies. Realizing Sam is desperate, Ruby also takes the opportunity to try and convince him that he needs to embrace his Yellow-Eyed Demon-given powers, because it's the only way to save Dean. Sam seriously considers the offer, until Dean rushes in and attacks Ruby. Ruby kicks Dean's ass, but loses her knife to him and finds herself ensnared under a devil's trap he'd prepared before her arrival. Ruby thinks Dean's crazy for not using the "bomb" inside Sam to eliminate Lilith and save his soul, but he won't listen. When Sam later suggests they consider listening to Ruby, Dean repeats, "We're not making the same mistake all over again." Sam doesn't understand what Dean means, so Dean explains that as he and their father have already sold their souls, he doesn't want to see Sam follow them down a path that can only lead to Hell.

Meanwhile, Lilith is relaxing by tormenting a nice suburban family. She has taken possession of ten-year-old Zoey Fremont and killed her babysitter. Sam, Dean, and Bobby hop in their cars and head her way. During the drive, Sam tries to give Dean an if-you-don't-make-it goodbye speech, but Dean's not having any of that. Instead he blares Bon Jovi on the radio and they have a brotherly singalong.

When they're pulled over by a cop on the outskirts of New Harmony, Dean kills the officer without hesitation. He saw the demon's face under the possessed officer's human countenance — and he can identify other demons in human form too... because he's almost one of the damned himself. But at least Lilith doesn't know they're coming, since she's too busy "playing" with Zoey's family — and killing Zoey's grandfather for trying to escape.

Dean spots Lilith through the Fremonts' window, but doesn't want to kill a little girl. Sam and Bobby remind him that Lilith is dangerous to the whole world, not just to Dean, so they have to take her out while they can. Ruby reappears, having

Above
Dean dreams he is
being chased by
hellhounds.

mysteriously escaped the devil's trap. Then all the nearby neighbors come out. They're possessed, and chase Sam, Dean, and Ruby into the Fremont house. Meanwhile, Bobby rigs the sprinkler system to spray holy water, which keeps the demons at bay.

Sam almost kills Zoey, but Dean sees that she's not possessed anymore. Lilith has escaped! Ruby informs them that Lilith is too powerful to let a little holy water stop her. Distraught, Sam tells Ruby he's ready to embrace his powers, but she tells him it's too late — he can't just flip a switch. Dean tells Sammy one more time that he doesn't want him to risk his own soul, and he has to let Dean go. Dean apologizes for putting Sam through this pain.

A grandfather clock on the wall begins to clang, striking midnight. A hellhound arrives. It's invisible to Sam, but clear as day to Dean and Ruby. The threesome race into the dining room and block the door and window with goofer dust. Then Ruby demands the knife back, and Dean realizes that Ruby's body has now been possessed by Lilith! She throws Sam up against a wall and flings Dean onto the kitchen table. Sam tries to trade himself for Dean, but Lilith says he has nothing to bargain with. She kicks away the goofer dust and lets the hellhound in...

Dean screams in agony as the hellhound tears him apart, while Sam can only watch. Dean dies and Lilith turns her attention to Sam, engulfing him in searing white energy. But when she lowers her hand and the white light dissipates, Sam is still there, completely unharmed. He grabs the demon-killing knife and approaches

Above

Dean's nightmare eerily foreshadows his death.

Lilith, gaining confidence with every step. She tries to use her powers to throw him up against the wall again, but he is now fully immune to her. As he raises the knife to strike, Lilith evacuates Ruby's body and escapes. Sam drops to the floor and cradles Dean's head in his arms, devastated that his brother is gone.

Dean is in *Hell*. Meat hooks pierce his flesh and he's strung up by chains that lead off into infinite darkness. He's terrified and very much alone, screaming for his brother, for somebody — anybody — to help him...

SAM: Hey, Dean?
DEAN: Yeah?
SAM: You know, if this... if this doesn't go the way we want, I want you to know that—
DEAN: Nooo. No, no, no, no, no.
SAM: "No" what?
DEAN: You're not gonna bust out the misty "goodbye" speech, okay? I mean, if this is my last day on Earth, I do not want it to be socially awkward.

"I was really pleased with the finale," states creator Eric Kripke. "I'm not sure we had an extremely clear sense at the beginning of the season how specifically we wanted the season to end. We knew we wanted Dean's deal to come due, and pretty

sure we wanted to send him to Hell, but we also had the mythology about Sam and where that was going to go. I think it was probably going to be a much more climactic confrontation with Lilith, much more aggressive and warlike. Dean's deal and what was going to happen with Sam were going to dovetail together more. By the middle of the season, before the strike, we said, 'You know, the size of what we're talking about doing isn't going to work.' We were going to have Sam and Dean going to war to save Dean's life, and it was going to be this big thing. By the middle of the season we said, 'We can't afford it.'

"Then the strike happened, and when you're walking the picket line, you talk, and you say, 'We're probably not going to have time to talk about Sam's issues, so we're really going to have to focus on: Can we save Dean from Hell — yes or no? Let's really think about what we want that answer to be.' And everyone's feeling was, 'Well, yes... yes, we want him to go to Hell. And we don't want Sam to save him because everyone's going to expect that.' Not that going to Hell was unexpected either, because that's what was hanging over his head all season, but that was the bolder choice. That way we could leave things on a cliffhanger.

"I look back and I think my primary problem with the season two finale is it just ended and there wasn't that same drive into season three. I really wanted a season three cliffhanger, because I wanted people to be biting their nails. So we said, 'Dean

Above
Dean searches every supernatural book he can find for a way to break his deal with Lilith.

Above

Sam tries to convince Dean to ask Ruby for help.

hanging in Hell is a hell of a way to do that.'"

"Sam was bound and determined that he could find a way to save Dean," points out executive producer Robert Singer. "Hopefully the audience believed what Sam believed, so it was shocking when Dean didn't make it. 'Cause I don't think anybody really expected that..."

Jensen Ackles certainly didn't expect it. "I wanted them to go that way, but didn't think they would," he explains, "because it's a network, so I was afraid everybody would be like, 'That's taking it too far.' I think it was definitely the right decision, especially with the kind of show that this is and the story that we're telling. That's a testament to Eric's brilliance in that he's saying, 'Give them what they want in a way they don't expect.'"

"Nothing surprises me with what Eric does," remarks co-executive producer Phil Sgriccia. "Sometimes you think you're in his mindset and you go left and he goes right."

In other words, the people working on *Supernatural* have come to expect the unexpected, which is why prop master Chris Cooper feels the decision to send Dean to Hell "seemed inevitable, really." Set decorator George Neuman agrees. "In a way, I kind of expected it. I think they had to in order to keep the story fresh for season four. Something critical like that had to happen." Executive producer Kim Manners concurs as well. "I always had a feeling that the ballsy decision would be to go ahead and make Dean pay up on his deal. It was definitely the right thing to do. I think that if he'd weaseled his way out of it somehow, it would've been a big letdown to the story. He had to pay the piper."

Composer Chris Lennertz took the decision to send Dean to Hell in his stride and immediately looked to season four. "My reaction was, 'How are you going to get him out of there?' And Eric was like, 'I don't know yet.' But I think it had to be done. One of the things *Supernatural* has done really well is the end of the season episodes.

They've always been so strong and not just cliffhangers; they tie up loose ends while also giving you a springboard into the next season."

Location manager Russ Hamilton "would've preferred a visual standoff somewhere. Something with a little more bang at the end — a big knock down, drag out fight. That would've been really super-cool!"

Of course, we did get a super-cool fight earlier on between Dean and Ruby... and since Lilith took over Ruby's meat sack for the climax, it would've been redundant to have another drag-out fight. And how comfortable would viewers have been watching Dean and Sam get into a knock-down brawl with the little Fremont girl?

"Some of my favorite scenes in this season were in 'No Rest for the Wicked', when Lilith is terrorizing that family just because she's on vacation," Kripke says. "It was either an homage or a rip-off, depending on how kind you're being to me, to *The Twilight Zone* episode 'It's a Good Life', with Bill Mumy, in which an all-powerful child terrorizes the adults around him. There's a scene when Lilith comes down and she's just coated and slicked with blood because their dog Freckles was mean to her. Then the family has to pretend to be happy because if they seem upset she's gonna get angry at them. I was laughing when I wrote those scenes. Parts of that episode were just so hard to write, and then all those scenes of her terrorizing her family I wrote in

Above
Bobby makes sure Sam and Dean don't go after Lilith without him.

DID YOU KNOW?

Zoey Fremont's name is a reference to *The Twilight Zone* character Anthony Fremont, the all-powerful little boy played by Bill Mumy, in 'It's a Good Life'.

five minutes each because they just came right out and were just so fun."

"A friend of mine was an actor in that *Twilight Zone* episode," composer Jay Gruska shares, "so it was fun to score the scenes with the evil kid. It's always fun to make evil kid music, and there were a couple of scenes where you're playing a little kid sound but it's absolutely sinister, so you can play something on the high register of a toy piano or something like that. Then with the right sort of low approach underneath it, you can really make a texture that's so great because you have that childlike quality and innocence, but it's ten times as creepy. I love to do that; it just brings out the twisted part of me.

**RUBY: Oh? So you're just too stupid to live, is that it? Then fine! You deserve Hell. I wish I could be there, Dean! I wish I could smell the flesh sizzle off your bones. I wish I could be there to hear you scream!
DEAN: And I wish you'd shut your piehole, but we don't always get what we want.**

"*The Twilight Zone* episodes were all brilliant, so they were sort of collectively in my head, but there was no specific quote musically intended or done," explains Gruska. "The truth is that no matter what preconceived notion I might have from reading a script or being told about something, what really makes me click is

Below
Lilith takes over
Ruby's body and
subdues Sam.

looking at the picture, because the scenes just ask for what they want, especially in *Supernatural*. Also, I think Eric is a big fan of silence as a scary device as much as music, and he's right on the money with that. A lot of times we might write something for a scene and it ends up getting pulled out at the mix. But you have to try it, twist and turn your way through it, and say, 'Alright, everybody's got the same goal: what makes the episode work and what makes it rise to the highest level it can be.'"

"I thought Lilith was a really effective villain," states Kripke. "Lilith was a cool demon to do," agrees Gamble. "Doing her as a demon that likes to possess little girls was interesting. Not so much that she is a child, but that she likes to possess little children. I think that's creepy and kind of molesty, honestly. She evolved into a woman, though."

Above

Dean recognizes Lilith inside Ruby's body.

That evolution truly impressed executive producer Kim Manners. "When Katie Cassidy made the turn from Ruby to Lilith, I thought she was just astounding in her portrayal," he says. Jared Padalecki was equally impressed. "Katie was great. She's a lot of fun to work with and be around, and I was really sad that we lost her."

Hamilton looks back on filming 'No Rest for the Wicked' with fond memories, but for different reasons. "That was the most rewarding episode we've ever done on this show," he feels, "just by the nature of where we were. We were in a full cul-de-sac of million dollar homes. There were sixteen houses, and we put every single homeowner up in a hotel, so we literally owned the whole cul-de-sac for two full nights. We went all night to sun-up. It was so challenging to organize, but it was so rewarding because at the end of it there were no complaints — not one single complaint. It was just so cool."

Despite organizing this great location, it still did not fit exactly the way they needed it to for every shot. "When Sam and Dean were in the window of the vacant house across the street watching the grandfather fall dead, they weren't actually

MUSIC

'Wanted Dead or Alive' by Bon Jovi
'Carry On Wayward Son' by Kansas

Above

Lilith attacks Sam with a blast of demonic white energy.

anywhere near that," Hamilton reveals. "They were on a two-story piece of scaffolding on a driveway across the street, looking through a fake window. When you're looking at them, they're actually in the basement of the house across the street, but we tied it together. Kim's vision of what he wanted, and the resiliency of the crew to make everything work, just made it a fabulous episode to be a part of."

Art director John Marcynuk loved working on the episode, too, but he had some trepidation when he first read the outline for the season finale. "When I read that, I said, 'Well, this is going to be hard,' because defining Hell is a difficult thing. I mean, if you ask fifteen different people what Hell is, you'll get at least fifteen different responses. We did some research, and it's amazing how many different images you can find of Hell. Chains and people being ripped apart are big ones, so what we came up with was good, but personally I think we could've made it a little more mysterious and dark. My opinion is, the vaguer the better, because you let the imagination take over. People have different fears, and Hell's such a personal torment."

"There was a lot of discussion about what exactly we see of Hell, because any version of Hell is really difficult to execute on our budget," explains Kripke. "Originally, Dean was going to be in some kind of really nasty, bloody slaughterhouse, hanging from meat hooks. You were going to see these dark shadows fall over him and he was going to scream... So it was going to be this manageable Hell, but the more Kim and Ivan and I talked about it, we started to say, 'Well, if we're going to show Hell, we should at least show one epic glimpse of Hell.' Then Ivan seemed excited to execute it and to give the audience just a glimpse of the size of this place, and so hanging from meat hooks in a slaughterhouse became hanging in the center of a million-mile web of chains rather than hanging from one chain in a room."

"We wanted to avoid the fire and brimstone aspect of Hell," adds Manners. "We wanted to come up with kind of an Escher-esque image, something we could afford to computer-generate. I think the shot worked really well. We just hung Jensen in a harness, and we had a prosthetic meat hook in his shoulder and one in his stomach, and the rest were CGI. We had him spread out and hung with some chains that led away from his body, and the rest of that was all just artwork."

"Any time you create a virtual environment, what makes that difficult is when you have a big camera move, because you are locked into that camera move," explains visual effects coordinator Ivan Hayden. "[For that sequence] we have Jared holding Jensen, then we go to Jensen's face and we push into the eyeball, then we transform out of the eyeball into this amorphous Hell, and you fly through Hell and end up seeing Dean in Hell, screaming. At the moment we see Dean, we're locked into what the practical camera motion is going to be.

BOBBY: Well, you got just over five hours to go. You're piercing the veil, Dean. Glimpsin' the B-side.
DEAN: Little less New Agey, please.
BOBBY: You're almost Hell's bitch, so you can see Hell's other bitches.
DEAN: Thank you.
SAM: Well, that'll actually come in handy.
DEAN: Oh, well, I'm glad my doomed soul's good for something.

"We had Kim shoot what he wanted with the crane and rotating camera moving toward Jensen's face to get his action. At the same time, I had a B-camera set-up rotated on its end so it's the vertical frame — so if you played it on your TV it would look like Jensen is sideways," continues Hayden. "What we ended up using was the B-camera for the whole front end of the shot, so we could re-time the camera move so that it could be more what Eric [Kripke] and Bob [Singer] wanted it to be. Then we put the tail end of Kim's rotating shot in the action, so what the director wanted would still be present in the shot.

"Originally we talked about doing a twelve- to thirteen-second shot, and it ended up being thirty-five seconds. Thirty-five seconds of HD film to render alone is huge! Plus, we had to make up the CG chains, paint out the wires, and time it into the

DEMONIC OMENS

During the filming of 'No Rest for the Wicked', key hair stylist Jeannie Chow noted some very odd weather patterns. "It was a really unusual filming day," she relates. "We were filming out in the south Surrey, White Rock area, and we had one day where it was really hot summer weather that turned into strong winds, then torrential showers, and then it snowed on us! Halfway through the scene it actually snowed — not little flakes, either, but giant dollar coin-sized flakes. It was when all the demons were coming, and there always seems to be a huge weather change when the demons come."

Above

Dean is actually dead... and his soul's in Hell.

lightning strikes. We built in practical lightning effects on the day so that Kim and Serge could be sure to have it the way they wanted it, but it slaves us into the frequency of the lightning, meaning we have to reverse-engineer the randomness of that lightning so it plays all the way through. We had ten days to do that whole thing. We called it the Hell Shot."

It was definitely hell for Jensen Ackles. "Out of the sixty episodes that we've shot, that was the most physical pain I've been in for one shot. I showed up at five in the morning to start a four-hour prosthetic application with the hooks in my side, neck, wrists and ankles. They bring me on set and they've got five wires wired up so they hook into my wrists and ankles. Then I put a belt on, cinched it really tight, and they piped me right in the back of the belt. I had five guys pulling me up and just basically quartering me. I was probably about thirteen, fourteen feet in the air, just hanging

THIS ONE'S FOR THE DOGS

"We pulled a prank on Jared Padalecki," shares costume designer Diane Widas. "He has these two big, beautiful dogs. At Old Navy they had dog costumes, and I thought it would be funny if we put the costumes on his dogs. They were western-type shirts, kind of like what he wears. I gave the costumes to the girls that have access to the dogs, and they put the outfits on the dogs. The boy dog only tolerated the bandana, but the girl dog actually didn't mind having the pink cowboy shirt on! I guess Jared didn't really think it was very funny though! 'My dogs don't wear clothes!' So he was dissing me, saying that I can dress him but I can't dress his animals — but it was the best prank!"

Above
Sam can't believe his
brother is dead.

there. Most of the weight was on my belt. The harness slipped past my jeans' belt and the metal buckle dug into my hip so I had all hundred and ninety pounds of myself basically resting on this buckle that was pinching into my hip, and I had to hold it there for five minutes, which is a really, really long time when you're suspended by one wire. So that was really tough. In fact, at the end of the shot, the big crane came up and started spiralling in and finally got to my face and they yelled, 'Cut.' As they were lowering me, I had tears rolling down my face, partially because of the scene but more because of the pain! It sucked, but it turned out to be a pretty cool shot."

"We went three or four takes before we got the one that we liked," states Manners. "We torture these kids. Thank God they're young and in shape, because they've done some things that most actors wouldn't do. Both of these kids will do anything — they'll go through glass — because they're nuts."

While the boys undoubtedly have fun doing their own stunts, Padalecki would most likely argue that the reason they're willing to go to hell and back for Manners and Kripke and everyone else is because they believe in the show they're working on. "I think season three truly set *Supernatural* up to be timeless," Padalecki asserts. "Whether we finish it in [season] four or five or whatever, I think what we accomplished in season three really set up the pitch for the homerun."

Looking ahead to season four, Ackles relates a conversation he had with Kripke: "'Okay, I'm in Hell now, so how are we gonna get me out?' And he replies, 'Haven't figured that out yet.' So I said, 'Let me know when you do, because I'm gonna be on pins and needles until you let me know.'"

A Closer Look At:
THE DEMON HIERARCHY

"There are all kinds of demons in season three," Eric Kripke points out. "We worked hard in season three to ground everything in demon lore. There are the Seven Deadly Sins and the devil-on-your-shoulder kind of demons who tempt people into drinking, prostitution, and abuse. Then there are demons who turn humans into witches. Every time we visit a demon we try to base it in some aspect of real history so we don't just spin off into pure fantasy.

"Nothing gives me more pleasure than writing one of the demons, because the demons can be so cruel and so funny — there's nothing they can't say. Every insult you've always wanted to say, the demon can just say it because that's what they do.

"We have an encyclopedia of demons," Kripke reveals. "In *Binsfield's Classification of Demons* (1589), Binsfield said the sins weren't just sins, they were classified by actual living demons." In the book, each of the deadly sins is paired with a demon who tempts people in ways associated with their namesake sin. "We took that idea and ran with it."

DEAN: All you demons have such smart mouths...
CASEY: It's a gift.
DEAN: Yeah, well, let's see if you're smiling when I send your ass back to Hell.

"We wanted to shade demons in a little different way," Bob Singer explains, "not just as black and white." It's no longer as simple as 'They're evil, we're good'.

"We couldn't just keep doing demons and their eyes turn black and they're evil and that's it," Sera Gamble agrees. "Our characters continue to evolve and deepen because the longer we're with them the more facets of them we get to know, so we revealed that demons used to be human. We introduced the character Ruby, who brought the idea that you can't just dismiss demons as things that need to be killed right away. They could be useful, and while fundamentally untrustworthy, there might be cause to trust them in a given situation."

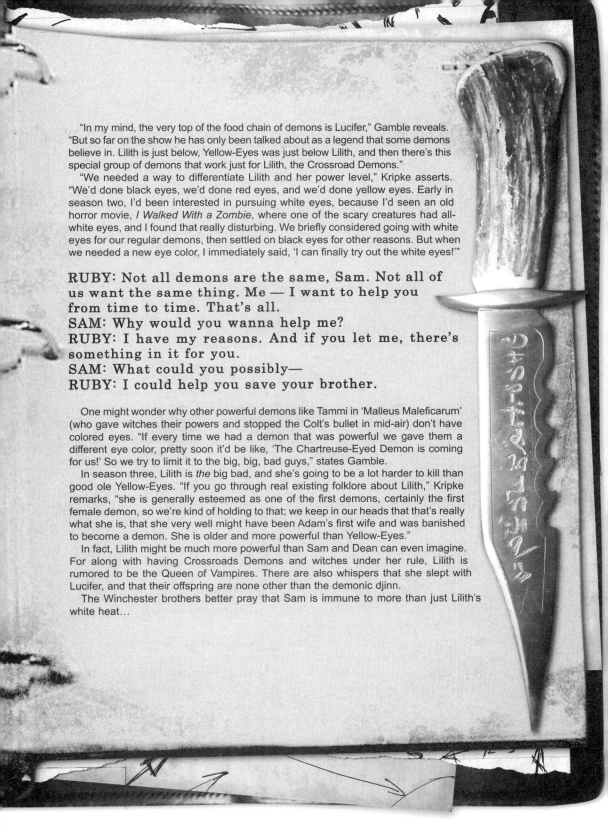

"In my mind, the very top of the food chain of demons is Lucifer," Gamble reveals. "But so far on the show he has only been talked about as a legend that some demons believe in. Lilith is just below, Yellow-Eyes was just below Lilith, and then there's this special group of demons that work just for Lilith, the Crossroad Demons."

"We needed a way to differentiate Lilith and her power level," Kripke asserts. "We'd done black eyes, we'd done red eyes, and we'd done yellow eyes. Early in season two, I'd been interested in pursuing white eyes, because I'd seen an old horror movie, *I Walked With a Zombie*, where one of the scary creatures had all-white eyes, and I found that really disturbing. We briefly considered going with white eyes for our regular demons, then settled on black eyes for other reasons. But when we needed a new eye color, I immediately said, 'I can finally try out the white eyes!'"

RUBY: Not all demons are the same, Sam. Not all of us want the same thing. Me — I want to help you from time to time. That's all.
SAM: Why would you wanna help me?
RUBY: I have my reasons. And if you let me, there's something in it for you.
SAM: What could you possibly—
RUBY: I could help you save your brother.

One might wonder why other powerful demons like Tammi in 'Malleus Maleficarum' (who gave witches their powers and stopped the Colt's bullet in mid-air) don't have colored eyes. "If every time we had a demon that was powerful we gave them a different eye color, pretty soon it'd be like, 'The Chartreuse-Eyed Demon is coming for us!' So we try to limit it to the big, big, bad guys," states Gamble.

In season three, Lilith is *the* big bad, and she's going to be a lot harder to kill than good ole Yellow-Eyes. "If you go through real existing folklore about Lilith," Kripke remarks, "she is generally esteemed as one of the first demons, certainly the first female demon, so we're kind of holding to that; we keep in our heads that that's really what she is, that she very well might have been Adam's first wife and was banished to become a demon. She is older and more powerful than Yellow-Eyes."

In fact, Lilith might be much more powerful than Sam and Dean can even imagine. For along with having Crossroads Demons and witches under her rule, Lilith is rumored to be the Queen of Vampires. There are also whispers that she slept with Lucifer, and that their offspring are none other than the demonic djinn.

The Winchester brothers better pray that Sam is immune to more than just Lilith's white heat…

SAM WINCHESTER

I lost my shoe.

"Season three was fun because we started out in season one with the premise of the show being that we were going into these urban legends and fairy tales and horrors that people grew up with and then we sort of strayed from that. So getting back to the Evil Santa Claus and the Seven Deadly Sins and the bedtime stories of Cinderella and the Three Little Pigs and stuff like that makes you go, 'Oh yeah — I know those.' It's getting back to the original purpose of striking at the heart of people who'd heard these stories all the time," Jared Padalecki points out. "It was really nice to get back to something that's more universally known."

But while the inspirations behind the stories got back to the show's roots, Padalecki's character, Sam Winchester, moved as far away from where he started as possible (without turning evil). "Obviously it's been a huge flip for Sam," Padalecki agrees. "In the pilot he wanted nothing to do with this world. He wanted nothing to do with his father, he wanted nothing to do with his brother, he just wanted to be a normal kid in college. Although I guess you're not normal if you're gonna be a lawyer — you gotta be pretty smart. But he wanted to live as normal a life as he could with the past that he'd had. He makes the switch after the pilot, after his girlfriend's gone, and he's back on the road with his brother, but even though he's committed to it, he's still fighting with, 'Why me? Why us? Why do we have to do this?'

"I think Sam was originally too pensive, too hesitant. When I started the show I was twenty-one, so it's not like I didn't think about things, but I was more from the cuff. Sam in season three is more like that — he's like, 'Well, okay, let's kill him.' Action first as opposed to really thinking it out. So whereas from an acting standpoint maybe I'll be forced into the position to think more, the character has been forced into the position to think *less*, to just trust his instincts. So in that way Sam's become a little bit more like me, even though I've probably made the other switch. Other than that, I think he's fleshed out more. Sam's an emotional guy, I'm an emotional guy. Ultimately, I think he's become more like me.

"That's something that happens with great writers. They get to know you, get to know your style, get to know what you like, and get to know what you're good at," continues Padalecki. "And you're good at what's like you, because in television we do [multiple pages per day], so you just infuse yourself into your work, it's accidental. A great writer will watch you on the show and kind of go, 'Huh, okay,' take a little mental note and write it into the next episode. I think the writers have taken cues from me, and I've taken cues from them, and I know what they want when they write certain things. There are times I'll see an ellipsis or I'll see something like, 'Sam lets

out a curt sigh,' and I'll think, 'Yeah, I know what they're after.'"

It was pretty clear what kind of emotional turmoil the writers were after when they killed off Sam and had Dean sell his soul to resurrect his brother. "In season three, with Sam having gone through what he went through with *dying* and then coming back to life, and realizing that his brother essentially doomed himself to an eternity in Hell to save him, he has a huge motivation to help his brother out the same way his brother helped him out," Padalecki explains. "He tries going to the Crossroads Demon and that doesn't work out, but he's really committed to solving this. From the pilot on through the first two seasons, the Yellow-Eyed Demon was our main go-to villain, but now the Yellow-Eyed Demon is gone and we've found out there are bigger and badder demons out there. Now the shit's really hit the fan."

Another big change in season three was the addition of the recurring characters, Ruby and Bela. "I feel the characters meshed really well with the show," Padalecki notes. "I remember at the very beginning, in the summer between season two and season three, I was going, '*Ohh*, they're adding *girls*... It's going to be *Gilmore Girls* all over again, or *One Tree Hill*.' Those are great shows, and they need their guy-girl relationships and romance, but it's been fun to just be dudes on a show in a badass car with some weapons and fight scenes and stuff. So I was like, '*Aww*, I know what girls mean, it means I'm going to have to take my shirt off again and I don't want to do that.' I hadn't met either girl, and I knew they'd probably be nice, but I just didn't know what they had to do with the story, how they were going to fit in.

"Then I met Katie Cassidy and Lauren Cohan and was like, '*Ah*, they're very sweet and very talented,'" Padalecki reveals. "They brought a whole new aspect to the show, a good dynamic to the show. Eric and the writers did it pretty seamlessly, and I think the girls fit in really well. I think Ruby had some great scenes and a great arc. As an audience member, I'm wondering, 'What's her deal?' With Bela, I was thinking, 'She stole the Colt? What the hell does she want with it? She's not a demon hunter. Did she sell it to Lilith? Or is she being possessed by a demon?' No one knew what was going on."

Once Bela stole the Colt, Dean seemed pretty tempted to actually kill her. Would the brothers ever

cross that line? "We've struggled with that in several episodes, about if someone doesn't know they're evil, or if someone's not evil, or someone's human and there's still good in them, then who has the power to be judge, jury, and executioner? Do we hold that power? Or can we only do that to a purely evil demon or spirit, something that's just out there to kill? Bela hadn't killed anyone — that we knew of — so we didn't really have the right to stop her."

In the end, they didn't need to play executioner, as Lilith's hellhounds handled that task nicely. Padalecki was surprised when he found out Bela's fate, but not nearly as taken aback as when he learned Dean would not be saved from the pit. "I didn't believe it," Padalecki exclaims. "I was like, 'What the hell?' I was so surprised, because it being *Supernatural*, there's always some clever way out. But I was relieved, too, and I'm glad they did it because it was what people least expected. Plus, otherwise Dean would've been the only Winchester not to die, so I'm glad he got to die!

"It was one of those situations that happens every finale, where I wanted to tell my family, tell my buddies, 'Dude, they're killing him!' But at the same time I didn't want to tell them because I wanted them to see it. I wanted to talk about it, but I had to wait until it came out."

As big as Dean's twist was, what Padalecki wanted to talk about even more was how Sam is apparently immune to Lilith's terrifying demonic white light. "I don't know the specifics, but Sam is powerful against Lilith. That's why she was so scared of him and why she was so freaked out. Good for Sam — what a badass!"

DEAN WINCHESTER

What do you want me to do, Sam? Huh? Sit around all day writing sad poems about how I'm going to die. Well, you know what, I've got one. Let's see, what rhymes with: Shut up, Sam!

"Each season is different from the last," Jensen Ackles comments. "Not just with the characters' motivations, and not just with the storylines behind the characters, but the individual episodes — they kind of take on different shapes and different forms. There's definitely a tone of the show that changes and evolves as well from season to season.

"I feel like, as far as Dean goes — because that's really all that matters in the show — this year has been less emotional for him." Being doomed to go to Hell is less emotional for him? "Yeah. The first year it was getting his brother back and finding his dad, and wanting his family to be together, with solidarity between the brothers and with their dad. It was very emotional when they all met up and were finally hunting together again. And then season two, he loses his father in the very beginning and he's got to deal with that, especially with finding out that John traded his life to save Dean. That really ate him up, there was a lot of emotion swirling around with that, as well as with what his father told him about Sam... And then Sam dies! So now in season three, he's made a deal, he's traded his life for his brother — he's content with that. It's made him a little numb this year to all of the emotional stuff.

"Hell, as an actor, it's easier to play. Just show up on set and wield some guns and kick some ass. No popping out tears or anything like that." At least, not until 'Dream a Little Dream', which features one of Dean's most emotionally powerful scenes, in which he argues with his doppelganger about being doomed to go to Hell... and then later tells Sam that he doesn't want to die. "You start seeing it toward the end of the season," Ackles concurs. "Deep down he's like, 'I don't want to go.'

"Truth is, I think he was scared shitless. I think no matter how much of a front he put on, no matter how much bravado he tried to have in front of his brother, it was all just a show to mask his terror. I think that kind of ultimate sacrifice is something he knew he had to make, but he definitely didn't want to go to Hell."

Now Bela, on the other hand, Dean would have been happy to send her there himself. "She's been a nice thorn in their sides," Ackles remarks. "Would he have killed her? Yeah, it may have come to that. It may have come to, 'Okay, look, she's messing everything up too much and people are getting hurt, innocent people are suffering. She's gotta go.'" So what happens if she escapes from Hell? "I don't know. Maybe she turns a corner and she's like, 'You know what, guys, I think saving people the way you do will really satisfy me. I want to hop in the back of the Impala and roll down the road with you.' That could happen," he deadpans. "I'd love to see what happens with that.

DID YOU KNOW?

When Jensen Ackles played Eric Brady on *Days of Our Lives*, his onscreen mother, Marlena, was once possessed by the Devil.

Maybe she and Bobby Singer could team up. That'd be kind of cool."

Apparently Ackles would find any excuse to have Jim Beaver's Bobby on the show more. "Absolutely." Not that there was any lack of great Bobby moments in season three. "I was thrilled about that," Ackles enthuses. "Jim's such a great guy and a fantastic actor. We joke about it, because the network that we're on is definitely skewed toward a younger audience, and here's this older guy coming on with the grizzly unshaved beard, but it works so well for the show, as opposed to getting some young buck to take his shirt off all the time."

Of course, there are countless female fans who would be quite happy to see Ackles take his shirt off all the time. The writers aren't likely to make that the norm, but maybe Ackles could just improvise and streak across camera... "Most of the improvising that we do is slapstick, jackass tomfoolery, so it's pretty much just for the outtake reel," Ackles reveals. "The writers know us, and they know how we speak, so we don't have to do a whole lot of improvising or a lot of paraphrasing. They write for us because they know how we would say certain things and how we would respond in certain situations, so we've been fortunate enough to be able to stick to the script and sound and feel normal and correct. But we do throw in little things here and there, and if it's something big, we'll call Eric up and be like, 'Hey, dude, for me, this just sounds better. What do you think?' He'll usually say, 'Yeah, man, if you're feeling it, then just go with it.'"

One thing that Ackles feels about Dean is that the character's less like the actor than he was in season one. "In season one, we were more similar because I was relying on my instincts to interpret the story. Whereas now I go back and I watch and I see what's working and what isn't and then it becomes, 'Oh, well, Dean wouldn't do that, so don't do that.' Or, 'Dean would do this or do that.' I'd say we've separated more, but we still share a lot of similarities. The more the story continues, the more of a character Dean becomes." For example, Ackles claims if he was in Dean's position, with one year left to live, he wouldn't live it so recklessly and, uh, promiscuously. "Dean's a little more of a roughneck than I am. I'd probably just blow all my money on my family and friends and try to spend as much time with them as possible."

Not that Ackles thinks Dean needs to change in any way. "Looking back, I think I'd make the same choices for Dean. I still have the same instincts, and I still interpret stuff very similarly. But I'd say where I've become improved as an actor would be technically; knowing more about lens sizes and camera angles and being aware of lighting and camera placement and this and that. Having that kind of mental knowledge become second nature to the performance is what I've improved most on."

Ackles also thinks Jared Padalecki has improved since season one. "I definitely think he's a better actor," states Ackles. "And the technical side of acting as well, that's why we work so well together. We know each other well enough that if I'm leaning this way, he knows that they can't see me behind him, so he immediately leans the opposite way. It's just that thing that happens while we're performing that most people would be like, 'Why is he leaning that way? What is he doing?' But he instantly knows, and vice versa."

Of course, the technical side of leaning the right way is probably the furthest thing from fans minds at the end of season three. Most likely, they reacted to Dean going to Hell in much the same way as Ackles' family. "My mom did not like it," Ackles exclaims. "Nor did my grandmother. They were asking, 'What's going to happen? How are you going to get out?' And I'm like, 'I don't know! They don't tell me anything!'

"I think sending Dean to Hell was the right choice," states Ackles. "I think there were too many times that Dean saved Sam or Sam saved Dean. You never want to get the audience to a point where it's thinking, 'Okay, here's a big bad situation, they're going to get out of it — they always do.' So I think it was great that Eric's attitude was, 'Guess what? Screw you guys. He's not getting out of this one. He's going to Hell!'" ✐

RUBY

I'm the girl that just saved your ass.

When Katie Cassidy went in to audition for the role of Ruby, she'd recently filmed the movie *Live!* in which she costarred with *Supernatural* alumnus Jeffrey Dean Morgan (John Winchester), so one might assume she could've called him up and asked for a referral to get past the initial stages of the sometimes-arduous audition process. "No, I had to audition for it," states Cassidy. "I know they tested other girls. Then they played my tape for the studio and the network. I went through the whole process." As it turns out, she couldn't have called Morgan even if she'd wanted to. "It's so sad, I lost my phone and all my contacts right after we wrapped. He's a sweet guy, and I know I'll run into him soon and we'll catch up."

Surprisingly, Cassidy originally auditioned for the role of Bela Talbot. "I went in for that, and then they had me go back in that same day, three hours later, for Ruby," Cassidy reveals. "It was a really crazy week because I was waiting to hear on two other projects I was up for, but if they wanted me, I was going to turn down the other projects." Thankfully, they did want her.

"It's great, but it's hard coming on to a new show in its third season," Cassidy admits. "Everybody's sort of already a family... but they welcomed me into their family. They made sure I was included, and they made me feel like I'd been there the whole time. It's just awesome working with Jared and Jensen. They're really sweet guys. Everyone you talk to will tell you the same thing, but it's true — they're so sweet, they're so welcoming. Jensen is cool, he's great. And Jared is a big goofball. Jared and I have this banter back and forth, which is funny."

Padalecki is known for his great sense of humor — and his practical jokes. Cassidy found herself a target on more than one occasion, the first being the most memorable. "I had this scene with ketchup where I squeeze it really, really, really hard and put a bunch of it on my plate. Well, I did that on the third take — and it was my third day on set and I was still pretty new — and somebody had unscrewed the ketchup bottle a little bit and left it so that when I squeezed the ketchup out, the ketchup went shooting all over me and my plate and my jacket. I was so embarrassed! But I was trying to basically just go with it. Jared was like, 'Wow, that's a lot of ketchup.' Then everyone sang 'Happy Birthday' to me, because if somebody breaks something or messes something up or gets a prank pulled on them, they all sing 'Happy Birthday' to you. I still don't really know if Jared did it or not. I don't even know if somebody planned it. Jared said, 'I didn't do that...' but then he said, 'Welcome to the family.' It was really embarrassing, but it was funny."

Despite the constant injections of levity into the atmosphere on set, Padalecki and Ackles are always consummate professionals when they need to be. "They know what

they're doing, and they get down to it," Cassidy agrees. "They're really hardworking, nice guys."

Cassidy had to work hard on the show, too, of course, particularly with learning new skills, such as fighting like a demon hunter. "It was crazy... taking kickboxing non-stop. I'd never done it before. As soon as I got to Vancouver they put me with a personal trainer so that I could learn how to kick some ass! [In the beginning] I was in it for six days a week. I used to be a competitive gymnast and wanted to build back those muscles and look pretty tough. By the later episodes you see me get some bulk."

Cassidy brought that same attitude to her character. "The character's completely different than anything I've ever played," she relates. "Ruby's a tough chick. She's a demon who's also a demon hunter. I created scenarios in my head of what would inspire her to do this. There are moments where I gave her that little spunk where it's kind of funny. It's like Sharon Stone's character in *Basic Instinct* — she's very manipulative, she uses her sexual energy to get guys to do things. I'm not saying that Ruby by any means sexually made guys do anything, but the sense you have with Sharon's character is that she's always in control. She always has the power, and there's this mystery about her. I also found inspiration thinking about how hardcore Angelina Jolie is in her action roles. Because, for my character at least, it was more like an action thriller kind of thing, which was really cool."

She hopes the female fans found her to be cool, too. "I just think it's good for the females out there to see another female literally physically kicking people's asses and taking care of herself. For me, when I see that type of character in a movie or on television, I'm just like, 'That chick is awesome!' I hope everybody has the same response to me as I do to those people. I don't want to inspire women to start fighting or anything, I just wanted to portray a strong, independent woman. I hope they like to watch girls kick some boys' asses… because there's a lot of that going on."

Yet, as great a fighter as Cassidy's Ruby is, what stands out even more is how she appears to always be scheming. "Ruby definitely loves to manipulate — she's always ten steps ahead of everybody else. She's got it together, she knows what she wants, and she knows how to get it. She can just work these boys so well."

It's no surprise then that Dean found Ruby extremely annoying. And Cassidy admits that she's been known to be annoying in real life… so much so that she was nicknamed 'Bug'. "It's true. My family and close friends call me Bug or Katie Bug. To be honest with you, I've had the nickname since I was young, and I don't even know if my mom knows where it came from. I guess when I was younger I was this really hyperactive kid. My mom said that once I could walk I was running around like crazy and running into walls. So maybe I was annoying and I bugged my parents so they came up with the name Bug."

Despite the fact that Ruby's "meat suit" is definitely dead at the end of season three, Cassidy "couldn't be happier" with the time she got to spend on *Supernatural*. Though she isn't willing to speculate on what's next for the character, she says "I'm sure they've got something extravagant planned for Ruby. She's always full of surprises." 🖋

BELA TALBOT

We're all going to Hell, Dean. Might as well enjoy the ride.

"I actually went in to read for Ruby," Lauren Cohan reminisces. "Then I went back a second time for Bela, and they asked me to read her with an English accent. When I met with casting, I didn't really think that much about it though, because I went in at the end of a long pilot season. So when I got a call-back to meet creator Eric Kripke, it was very exhilarating, and when I left that meeting, I felt like it was definitely happening!"

Thing was, she didn't know exactly *what* was happening. "I only had about two pages of script," she reveals, "so I really didn't know what Bela was about. I actually wasn't aware of much to do with my character until right at the last minute. I guess it was to protect the show and to keep news away from fans and such. I didn't even know she was going to be a nasty person! Then, on the night of The CW up-fronts, Eric was like, 'I think I should probably tell you more about your character, 'cause you're going to be interviewed.' I said, '*Yeah*, that would be cool.' So he gave me a good spiel about Bela, and then on I went."

Cohan probably would've been well prepared for the interviews, anyway, having just watched the first two seasons on DVD. "They sent me the DVDs when I booked the gig, but I didn't realize how scary *Supernatural* was until then. I had to wait for people to come home and watch it with me because I have a really weak stomach for scary things," she confesses with a laugh.

Between honing up on the show, listening to Kripke's spiel, and reading the scripts, Cohan developed Bela's personality. "I think Bela was just a young woman trying to make a living and find some kind of reason in her world. She was a little damaged. I tried to bring an essence of her putting on a front that wasn't really her true self. I think that Bela definitely had to create a persona that protected her from real strong connections most of the time. I feel that as we came to know her more, she became more interesting."

"Interesting" is probably not one of the words the Winchester brothers would use to describe Bela. Yet, despite Bela's antagonistic relationship with the boys, Cohan thinks "she would have loved to be able to have a normal relationship with them, a normal friendship, to even be on their side. But I think she had grown accustomed to living defensively and not really opening herself up or making herself vulnerable. She would have loved to go around fighting evil with those boys... She did help them a little bit more in the end, and I definitely think she had fits of conscience when she kept stealing from them and impeding their progress."

Another sign that the hate-hate relationship could easily have veered into love-

hate territory was when Bela suggested to Dean in 'Red Sky at Morning' that after the ball they should go have "angry sex"... Cohan laughs when asked if she thinks Dean took Bela up on her offer off-screen. "The possibility of things is always more interesting than the actual fulfilment, I think," she professes.

Apparently, in Sam's mind, anything is possible... even sleeping with the woman who shot him. Cohan thinks that scene in 'Dream a Little Dream of Me' was "really funny". Even off-screen, the scene was more humorous than romantic. "Jared was so protective for doing that whole thing," Cohan recalls. "He was so sweet. He was like, 'Okay, so if you feel uncomfortable at any time, just give me a signal and I'll make sure that we stop and we do what needs to be done so that you feel comfortable.' It was quite amusing to be doing a sex scene with somebody who was acting so brotherly and sweet and protective. I think he was more nervous than I was!"

Of course, amusing things happen on the *Supernatural* set all the time, as Cohan attests. "There was the time when we were in a rundown apartment and there were rabbit traps and mouse traps and all kinds of wooden traps everywhere to make it look shabby. Jared kept trying to get everybody to put their fingers in the mouse trap. He kept saying, 'Hey, come here, hold this. Jensen, come here...' Then he trapped his fingers in it, which was kind of funny."

They're infamous for their pranks, but Padalecki and Ackles also have a reputation for trying to make other actors mess up or laugh during their own camera coverage. "They did that to Katie," Cohan confides. "She had this habit where she went to her mark and did this little pose. She said that when she'd be going to her mark on her coverage, Jared and Jensen would stand there and put their hands on their hips and do the Katie pose. She kept telling me she couldn't concentrate.

"Then there was a time where I had to say the line, 'He was tried in a kangaroo court and hung,' and I probably had twenty takes of this thing. Jared and Jensen kept mimicking me after I said each one, which was just making me completely unable to say it, so I was like, 'He was a kangaroo... He was tried as a kangaroo... He was a hung kangaroo...' It was very funny."

There was also the apple box incident. "I was shooting a scene and there was a close-up of us and I was sitting on an apple box," Cohan explains. "The camera was very close and I was supposed to stand up as the camera moved back and walk away. So I start the scene, I'm sitting on an apple box, then I stand up, and they pull the box away. But I fluffed my line and said, 'Nope, don't stop rolling, I'll just go straight away again,' and I didn't know that the apple box had already been taken away… so I walked back to sit down and fell down on my butt! It was pretty funny. I had to spend a couple of weeks living that one down."

Considering how much fun Cohan had on the *Supernatural* set, it's no surprise that she was sad that they killed her character off. However, she was not surprised that Bela only lasted one season. "Not after I noticed the fan reception of her," Cohan admits. "I have to be honest, I found the negative fan response a little overwhelming. Katie and I both felt that. It was like, 'Give us a chance!' It's very much the boys' show though, and I can see that fans would be afraid our coming on as recurring characters would change the dynamic of it, and that it was a protectiveness more than anything. I get that. But it was sad, because in the sequence of us actually making the show, I think people were just starting to warm up to her [in the episodes on the air] as she was leaving [in the episodes being filmed]."

The silver lining is that Cohan enjoyed the way Bela's arc wrapped up. "I thought it was really nice because we finally had some revelation into her, and it was quite sympathetic from an audience perspective. I also thought it was scary and mysterious, and suitable. Bela getting ripped to shreds by hellhounds is a cool way to go! Plus, the fact that you never see it, you just hear the growling of the hellhounds — that was haunting."

"I'd love to return," Cohan submits. "It'd be really fun. Bela is quite clever — maybe she could finagle her way out of Hell, somehow. Maybe…" ✦

BOBBY SINGER

Just look out for your brother, ya idjit.

"At first Bobby was just a friend of Sam and Dean's dad who helped out in a given situation. Now, I think there's a real bond growing," states Jim Beaver. "It's weird, this surrogate father thing... It seems like with their real dad there was a lot of baggage, but with Bobby they don't have so much baggage."

Despite the continually growing bond between the boys and Bobby, they don't just go to him for fatherly advice. Bobby's help and experience as a hunter is invaluable. "I think he's really smart, but he also knows what he doesn't know," Beaver acknowledges.

One of the things that Bobby is an expert in is exorcisms, thanks to his obsession with demons following the uh, *accidental* death of his demon-possessed wife. "I'm a language freak," Beaver reveals, "and I've studied Latin, but it's hard to memorize because I only have a rough acquaintance with what the words mean. Most of the time they don't require us to memorize it, though — usually the prop guys will paste it into one of the books that we're supposedly reading."

Given the environment he works in, one might wonder if Beaver has ever considered memorizing the exorcisms anyway, just in case a real demon shows up on the set of *Supernatural*. "No," Beaver claims. "It would be a lot of fun to say yes, but the fact is, even when we're creeping around old dark houses, the camera crew and everybody is there, so there's like fifty guys you can't see all around us. On the set, there's always creepy atmosphere that is engineered for the benefit of the show, but the actual atmosphere is never creepy. It's about as quiet and eerie as your average airport terminal. I've never had any kind of supernatural experience on *Supernatural*..."

Although, one has to wonder if Beaver has a supernaturally lucky rabbit's foot, since Bobby's longevity is a rarity on a show known for killing off its great characters. Beaver feels this "happy accident" is influenced by his chemistry with Jared Padalecki and Jensen Ackles. "There's something in our real-life relationships that is reflected onscreen," Beaver believes. "We work really well together and I have a lot of respect for them — and I get a kick out of their antics. There's a constant lightheartedness on the set, and Jared and Jensen really lead that. Jared's got this god-awful fart machine, and every once in a while it just makes the entire soundstage unlivable. Fortunately that doesn't translate onto film, or there wouldn't be anybody watching the show! The cast and the crew give and take with each other a lot. I love it when the boys get into a physically confining space because usually somebody on the crew is gonna dump water on them or trap them or something like that. It's a very, very fun-filled set.

"It's a sweet gig." ✐

DID YOU KNOW?

Jim Beaver stars in the movie *Reflections*, which is reminiscent of the *Supernatural* episode 'Bloody Mary' in that it's about a woman who sees horrors whenever she looks into a reflective surface.

VICTOR HENRIKSEN

Don't you dare say demons. Let me tell you something, you should be a lot more scared of me.

Charles Malik Whitfield calls his time on *Supernatural* a "blessing", yet it started out like any other gig, where he "auditioned amongst many other actors. I read the material and said, 'Yeah, this is pretty cool.' The character is pretty no-nonsense and obviously relishes what he does. I was fortunate enough to get the call. It was really that simple."

In the same way that Agent Victor Henriksen relishes his job as an FBI agent, Whitfield relished "the fun of committing to a chief in command. It's the kind of role where you can cut people off midway in their sentence. It's really fun when you just cut somebody off of some important stuff and say, 'No, I think my stuff is more important.' That had weight to it, because in the normal day to day of how we interact with people, there's no way we would do that. It's almost like playing a villain."

While Henriksen was on the side of good, he did come off as a villain for his treatment of the show's heroes, as Whitfield experienced firsthand. "A friend of mine called me and was like, 'I hate you!' And I was like, 'Hello? You got the right number?' She said, 'You are on my show and how dare you chase those boys!' She was dead serious about 'Don't come on my show if you're not going to do anything good...' They are dedicated, wonderful fans. The show is so impactful."

Likewise, the brothers greatly impacted Henriksen's life. "He was definitely consumed by the job," asserts Whitfield. "His perspective was, this is what I do and this is how proficient I am in the way I capture people and shut them down... and these guys keep going right by me. It was a new benchmark for him. Yet, even though he was being trumped, he was able to see a lot of greatness and genius in what the Winchester boys were doing."

The dynamic of the hunters being hunted (by a human, no less) made for thrilling television, and at one point the writers considered making that a significant part of season three. "There were some talks of 'Hey, would you want to relocate to Vancouver? Do the show permanently?'" Whitfield reveals. "I said, 'Of course!' But they had to figure out where they wanted to take things and what they wanted to focus on..." In the end, Henriksen only came back once in season three, but that didn't diminish the role's importance to Whitfield. "My agent said, 'They want you to come back, but we have this movie set up that we don't want to throw out of balance...' and I was like, 'No, you lock in *Supernatural*!' I just have that much fun."

Which you'd think would make it all the more painful to have his character killed off, but Whitfield has a very Zen attitude. "I wasn't disappointed. I believe that everything that's good, it all too must end. We just embrace it in the moment.

I knew that I would truly miss hanging out with the guys, but I'll see them again..." Is that a hint that he'll be back as a ghost? "Anything's possible. I just take it for what it is. Working on *Supernatural* is definitely high up on my totem pole of wonderful experiences."

HARRY SPANGLER & ED ZEDDMORE

HARRY: Hey, aren't those the a-holes from Texas?

"I got who the characters were quickly," Travis Wester recalls of his audition for the Hellhounds (a.k.a. The Ghostfacers) in 'Hell House'. "They were the bumbling versions of *Supernatural*'s main characters. I just went in there and read for director Chris Long and executive producer Bob Singer... and they decided to pull the trigger on me."

"My experience was slightly different," A.J. Buckley reveals. "My agent tried to get me in and casting said, 'No, A.J.'s not right, he's too good-looking for these nerdy guys."

"That is not a problem for me!" Wester interjects.

"But one of my dear friends is David Nutter, who did the pilot," Buckley continues. "I called Nutter and said, 'Casting doesn't believe I can be this character — can you try to get me a pre-read or something?' So he made a call and the next thing you know, I had the appointment!"

As with the fated pairing of Jensen Ackles and Jared Padalecki, *Supernatural* could not have chosen a better couple of actors to play the Hellhounds. "We met at wardrobe," shares Buckley. "So for the two of us to click like we did was amazing. We just kind of fell right into it."

"My character, Ed Zeddmore, is the visionary of the group," Buckley points out. "He idolizes Captain Kirk [from *Star Trek*]. He tends to think he's a bit of a ladies man, but he's a total sham. He would be completely lost if he did not have Harry Spangler. Harry is the facilitator of his vision."

"Yeah, Harry's not a big idea guy like Ed is," Wester admits. "He sees himself as the implementation specialist. He's more comfortable exercising Ed's will than necessarily having any particular will of his own. He's very detail-oriented, very particular, fastidious, orderly, by the book, by the numbers..."

So, what exactly is Ed's vision? "Being known as the greatest ghost hunters of all time," states Buckley. "Ed and Harry laugh at Sam and Dean, who are hacks. We're the real deal."

Why did they change their name from Hellhounds? "Marketing," Buckley explains. "We did the research and what the chicks dug was Ghostfacers."

"It just sounds sexier," Wester adds.

"And as Facers," Buckley continues, "we ask the other Facers to look into their internal face and face that face and see if they can face other faces."

Perhaps the most important question is: How do you prepare for facing ghosts? "You can bring rock salt and shotguns, but..." Buckley begins and then Wester takes over. "All that nonsense is if you actually want to do something about the ghosts.

DID YOU KNOW?

Ghostfacers Ed and Harry's last names were chosen in homage to the characters Winston Zeddmore and Egon Spengler from the movie *Ghostbusters*.

Ghostfacers are about meeting a ghost and facing it, and then leaving it for future generations. I just wish Sam and Dean wouldn't be so disruptive with the supernatural. Leave some for the rest of us, you know?"

"Yeah!" Buckley exclaims. "Just keep on facing is all we have to say. Actually, *this* is our last comment: The Ghostfacers say, 'Stay razor.'" ✐

GORDON WALKER
Sam Winchester must die.

When we left Gordon in season two, he was being hauled off to jail... So how did he feel about getting outsmarted by Sam? "Bitter," responds Sterling K. Brown without hesitation. "He didn't think he was capable of being outfoxed. The fact that Sam got past both tripwires, then bested him in a fight, *and* had the savvy to have called the police beforehand to set Gordon up... that's more credit than Gordon would've given any Winchester brother. He's bitter, but at the same time, it's like, 'Game on.'

"Jail just focused him. He knew he had to make a pre-emptive strike and take Sam out before he obtained ultimate evil status." Gordon was so determined to accomplish his task that he broke out of prison. "I'd imagine someone of his resources had help from the inside," Brown muses. "He could've made a threat to the family of someone who's in a position to get him out. I think it probably went down like that."

His freedom was short lived, however, as he is soon turned into his worst nightmare: a vampire. "I felt so bad," Brown reveals. "Gordon became a vampire hunter because his sister got turned into a vampire and he had to kill her. So to have come full circle, to have become a vampire and turned an innocent girl into one, I was crushed. When I read the script, I screamed, 'No! Noooooo!'"

Brown went from screaming to crying when he found out Gordon was killed off. "I may have shed a tear," Brown admits. "I was sad. The *Supernatural* experience has been some of the most fun I've had in my career. Jared and Jensen are outstanding guys, and the city of Vancouver is absolutely beautiful. I really love the character, so if there's any way that Gordon can come back, I will be ready."

Gordon could always come back as a decapitated ghost carrying his head around. "If you've got to go, that's the way to go — wire to the throat. That was intense," Brown exclaims. "My wife watched it and was like, 'I don't like watching you die.' But I thought it was pretty cool. I felt like they did the character a great service in giving him a spectacular demise. I get kind of giddy over stuff like that, but my wife was a little disturbed... and more disturbed at the fact that I actually enjoyed it!" ✒

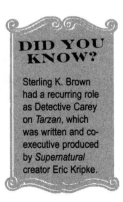

DID YOU KNOW?

Sterling K. Brown had a recurring role as Detective Carey on *Tarzan*, which was written and co-executive produced by *Supernatural* creator Eric Kripke.

Bela's apartment, where she sleeps "In silk sheets, rolling naked in money."

'The Magnificent Seven' magnificent motel room.

The safehouse, complete with sailing ship painting, from 'Red Sky at Morning'.

John Winchester's storage room, near Buffalo, New York, "a really interesting treasure trove of potential weapons".

Demons, including the Seven Deadly Sins, enjoy their newfound freedom in 'The Magnificent Seven'.

Demons beseige the sheriff's office at Lilith's command in 'Jus In Bello'.

THE TRICKSTER

You chuckleheads tried to kill me last time...
Why wouldn't I do this?

Richard Speight Jr. *is* the Trickster. He didn't even have to audition. "Casting called my agent and just offered me the role," Speight reveals. "I'd worked with [executive producer] Bob Singer before, and I'd done a lot of work with those casting directors, so I'm imagining they had a conversation where my name came up and they all nodded. It's one thing if someone says, 'Hey, you want to come play the guy that serves coffee?' But to get a shot at doing something like the Trickster, which is such a flippin' fun character, is great. I was thrilled that they trusted me to do it sight unseen.

"The thing I love about the Trickster is his unpredictability. You never know if he's screwing with Sam and Dean because he's trying to teach them something, or if it's just his way of killing time. A character like the Trickster leaves a lot open to interpretation, and I brought a wry humor to the guy. The road I've gone down with the character is to make it clear that no one enjoys the Trickster's work more than the Trickster. He thinks he's hilarious. He thinks he's a genius. That bold cockiness is a little bit of the Richard Speight touch. You gotta love a guy who loves his work as much as the Trickster does; there's something admirable in that, even if his work is making the Winchester boys squirm."

Playing the sweet-toothed Trickster in his first appearance, in season two's 'Tall Tales', made Speight himself squirm in his seat. "I had plenty of caffeine via chocolate. We shot that theater scene from a million different angles, and every time I was chomping away on candy bars. Even with a spit bucket, I was consuming a pretty good chunk of chocolate. Let's just say I didn't need any coffee that day..." Not that Speight wanted the theater scenes to wrap any quicker. "I want to go on record as saying I enjoy watching girls wrestle in their underwear," he deadpans. "The director was very persistent in covering that scene from every angle."

Speight obviously enjoys working on *Supernatural* and hopes to return. "The Trickster definitely led us to believe that's most likely the case, because his closing line was, 'That's for me to know and for you to find out.' That certainly indicates that there might be more mayhem afoot!" *⚡*

DID YOU KNOW?

One of Richard Speight Jr.'s first roles was in the 'It's My Party and You'll Die if I Want You To' episode of TV horror anthology series *Freddy's Nightmares*, based on the enduring film series *A Nightmare on Elm Street*, which influenced such *Supernatural* episodes as 'Dream a Little Dream of Me'.

MEET THE CREW: SPECIAL MAKEUP EFFECTS

"**W**orking on *Supernatural* is always exhilarating," enthuses Toby Lindala, head of special effects makeup. "As soon as we get a concept, we hit the ground running and do the best we can in about a week and a half, two weeks. I feed on that adrenaline, on that excitement.

"I like doing gags like sawing up Richard in 'The Kids Are Alright'. We did a false torso for him to fall back onto for a close-up shot of the saw entering his back. It had a neat spinning cable that we hooked up to a drill, as well as another cable that would cause that to arc up. It appears as though the blade was pushing into him and through skin on the inside of his shirt. Simple, but really effective. It was fun."

Speaking of fun, Lindala and his crew get to play with Jell-O on a regular basis! The Hand of Glory in 'Red Sky at Morning' was made from plastic bones and gelatin. "There's a neat trick that we do for a lot of desiccated skin where we use gelatin, which is a wonderful material because it's translucent like skin," Lindala reveals. "We can set the opacity at different levels, whatever the project calls for, but it's just Jell-O essentially, mixed with glycerin rather than water, so it creates this rubber. You can melt it in the double boiler or even a microwave. We make that in a negative mold of a hand, we lay in a little bit of latex first — like three stippled layers of liquid latex — and follow that with a layer of gelatin and tint it the way we want it, then we just make these thin skins and take those and stretch them around and glue them over the top of a posable medical skeleton and blend in pieces however we want. You can get a really organic feel to the wrinkling in the way you manipulate the skin on top. It's a simple trick that anybody can try at home."

Another great material for special effects makeup is silicone gel, which they got to utilize in 'Mystery Spot'. "We did a neat build for Jared Padalecki with a full torso piece for him, where he pulls the bullet out of the bullet wound and then stitches it up. We did it out of this silicone gel; it's nice, it really reacts to manipulation like skin. It was disturbing to watch, to see him reaching in and prodding around with forceps. It was fun to do, though. We just laid it on him and strapped it on like a corset. He actually did all the extraction of the bullet, as well as the stitching."

Lindala's favorite episode was 'Time Is On My Side'. "That was a really fun episode for us. Billy Drago is a really wonderful, gentle man. He brought a lot to the character. He really embraced the concept. He had a four-hour makeup. It's a torturous process. We did a lot of the stitching in advance, then we had to add on single stitches with glue and tweezers, kind of like putting on individual eyelashes. I think we had a total of about 120 stitches that we had to add on each day, and then it's about an hour afterward for clean up. We had four different distinct skin tones in

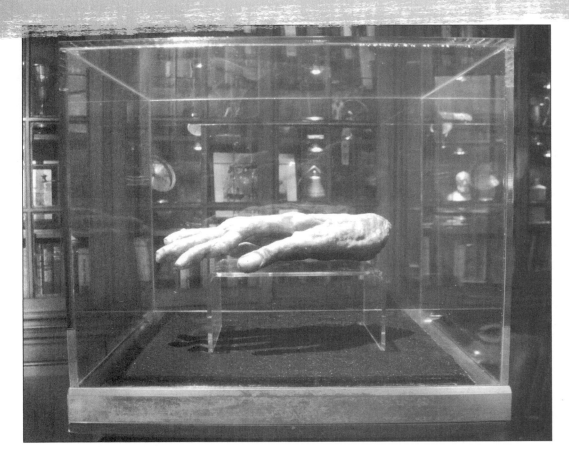

it, one of them being Doc Benton's own skin. That was one thing I was really happy with in the end. We tried to keep a sense of logic to the way that it went together so that if you looked at it and thought about it, you could tell what was him. We did some latex stipple around his left eye and the appliances that went around that were sculpted to a wrinkled texture, quite pale and pasty. With that same tone, we did latex stipple around his right cheek. That way, you also get maximum performance, since you don't have the limitation of covering his entire face in foam. It actually kind of enhances his movements, because rather than stretching out and pulling his skin taught, you do an appliance on a pulled position and let it relax back and it gives something more for any subtle movements."

There was nothing subtle, however, about the meat hooks tearing into Dean's shoulder and stomach in 'No Rest for the Wicked'. "That was a three-hour makeup, which is the longest we've had to work on Jensen," Lindala notes. "Dean in Hell was a pretty horrific image."

Fortunately, "horrific" is not the way Lindala would describe *Supernatural* overall. "There's just a really comfortable creative energy on the show. Working on it definitely is exhilarating." ✐

Above

The Hand of Glory, in all its glory…

Page 132 (clockwise from top left)

Lindala explains, "This is our 'drunk in taxidermy' (duplicating actor Tony Morelli) and 'salesman in taxidermy' (duplicating actor Dave Hospes) for 'Ghostfacers'." Jensen Ackles relaxes between takes with some of Freeman Daggett's party guests.

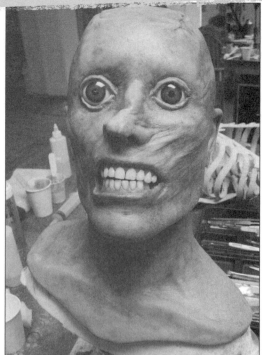

MEET THE CREW:
LOCATION MANAGERS

"I'm always amazed at how well they're able to find places in and around Vancouver that can pass for almost any place in America," says Jim Beaver. Location managers Russ 'Movie God' Hamilton and Paul Lougheed truly do an amazing job of finding perfect locations for filming *Supernatural*. So how do they do it?

"There's a lot of driving around, just looking," admits Hamilton. "We've been looking for a diner in the middle of nowhere since season one, episode one, and that just doesn't exist. We've been looking for a motel in the middle of nowhere. They don't exist. I mean, stuff "in the middle of nowhere" actually exists, but we can't go there because we have a studio zone, and we can't afford to go to those places to shoot. We're in a metropolis area, there is no middle of nowhere here. We have to find a controlled road where we can erect those sets, so we return to this one area, an old shut down military base. All the buildings are gone, it's just the road system still there."

Another middle of nowhere landscape that they can't find within the studio zone is a desert. "We do have smaller sand areas around the lower mainland," Lougheed points out, "but not to the extent of a desert. We do have deserts in British Columbia,

Below

Jared Padalecki stands at a crossroads on an old military base.

Above

Lauren Cohan approaches Jensen Ackles and Jared Padalecki on a cemetery set built on location in Heritage Park, Burnaby, BC.

but they're three hours away in the interior, and we don't go three hours away on this show. They've got rattlers and black widow spiders and the whole routine there; it's perfect for Arizona, but too far a drive."

"We've been back to many locations two or three times and you would never know it," asserts Hamilton. "You would never be able to tell unless you were watching the film really closely to see where it was, but you'd almost never know we're back in the same place. We have one of the best art departments going. They'll dress different chairs or dress different carpets or maybe shoot a different angle that we didn't actually see in the first one.

"It becomes more challenging to find places we haven't filmed at before. Because of the nature of *Supernatural*, we always have something different and unique to look for. It makes us have to up our game even more to find that really cool stuff that's out there. At that point you start thinking, 'What else can we turn into a spooky house? What can we turn into a spooky factory?' We revisit the same motel exteriors again and again too. We're now using backs of office buildings just so we have an exterior, or we're doing the interiors with a reverse outside the door just to make it look like there's something out there, but there never really is. There isn't a motel within a hundred miles that we don't know about."

"It all starts with breaking down the script," Lougheed explains. "I'll be the first person in Canada to actually read a script and I break it down into locations; all the

Above
Sam and Dean enjoy
the fresh air.

scene numbers, the page count, whether it's day or night, and a brief description of the scene. That way we figure out what's going to be in the studio and what's going to be an actual location. Traffic control, getting the permits, that's completely our thing. I can't show them a great-looking location and say, 'But you can't film there.' That's the death of a location manager."

"Eric and all the writers are great," states Hamilton. "If the location they're looking for doesn't exist and we say we can't do it as scripted, we'll get pages the next day changing it to the way we need it to work to fit the location, which is a blessing and another reason it's a great show to work on, because everybody does understand the process and everyone works together to make it a fun job."

"The profession can be fun and can be incredibly stressful," admits Lougheed. "We have to deal with the real world; we are the middlemen. We gotta win people over." To ease that stress, Lougheed says, "Russ loves to play practical jokes. Whenever we go into a location, particularly a house, it's common for everyone to take their shoes off, so Russ mismatched all the shoes, moved them all around, hid them here, hid them there, so when the survey came out of the house it was a total scramble. We're two opposite people, and that's why we get along. I'm more controlled and organized and Russ is off the cuff."

"It's challenging work," Hamilton notes, "and *Supernatural* is the hardest show I've worked on. But it's also the *funnest* show I've worked on."

MEET THE CREW: PROPERTY MASTER

I looked at the pilot and immediately fell in love with the show," recalls property master Chris Cooper. "For me, the props that are involved are pretty cool. In terms of making a living and being a props master, I'm doing stuff within a realm that's interesting to me. It's the kind of show I watch. For my department, it's really fun. It really is, 'Let's go play with our toys today.'

"An interesting part of this for us is the weapons cache and taking what was originally in there and building on it," Cooper continues. "My thing — and something that Eric Kripke's really into — is keeping it in a realm of reality, even though you can look into that trunk and pull pretty much any weapon out of there and it'll still be believable that it was hidden under something else. We eventually broke it down to six handguns, and then as we needed other weapons, they became part of the weapons

Below

A glimpse into the Impala's weapons cache.

Above

The Colt in its original
case with its original
bullets.

cache. I try to reuse as much stuff as possible, within what the directors want to do and what Eric wants us to do. Eventually we worked to the point where now Dean Winchester has a handgun that's specifically his handgun that he pretty much uses all the time. He's got a colt 1911, .45 calibre, it's fully engraved, it's got pearl handles. It's an awesome weapon. Sam has a handgun that's specifically his, too. Sawed-off shotguns play a big part, as well, and we have a specific sawed-off shotgun that Dean uses and one that Sam uses. The weapons cache is perpetually growing.

"The big prop from season one is the 'hero gun', the Colt," says Cooper. "It's an 1836 Colt Patterson, Texas — the first revolver ever made! Samuel Colt, the guy they talk about in the episodes, this was the first gun he ever conceived. He carved one completely out of wood while he was in the army, and when he finished his run in the army he hooked up with a company in New Jersey called Patterson, and they started producing what was the first revolver ever. We got a functioning replica from an Italian manufacturer. It's a ball and cap gun, so we built a new cylinder for it, and the cylinder takes regular cartridges basically — regular blanks. Then we engraved some Latin on the barrel: *Hear no evil*, and put the pentagram onto the handle. We took a lot of the finish off as well, to give it an aged look, like it's been around for a while. I love this weapon. From my point of view, having to come up with something like the Colt is just so cool.

"The journal is great, but it was created for the pilot, so there wasn't much creative input from my department here in Vancouver. We took the original and made a couple of them. We try to have at least two of everything no matter what it is."

Except for the Colt. And the curse box from 'Bad Day at Black Rock'. "We designed and built a curse box from scratch. Because of the iron factor with ghosts and stuff, I made the box that holds the rabbit's foot out of iron. It's the heaviest thing ever — if you open the lid, the whole thing tips over from the weight of it." Cooper wants it known that "no actual rabbits were killed for the show. We had to burn that rabbit's foot at the end, so obviously we needed several rabbits' feet for takes. But try to find a rabbit with its feet still on! That's the first thing that goes when they process rabbits. Plus, it had to be a big jackrabbit size. I have a number of sources where on any given day I can buy an eviscerated rat with one phone call from different taxidermies. We just call these guys up and tell them what we're looking for and it's like, 'Oh yeah, I've got three rabbits in the fridge...'

"A lot of that stuff I buy out of Hollywood, too, at a store called Necromance. They have a cool website. For 'Malleus Maleficarum', I couldn't find a rabbit carcass anywhere, so I rented that from this place in Hollywood. You want a horse that's been hit by a car? They've got it. And these are real taxidermied animals. They shipped the rabbit up to me, the rabbit worked on camera, then he went back home to Hollywood.

"For the props department, this show is simply awesome. The stuff we get to deal with, the stuff we get to create and build and play with... And then to have a couple of actors that actually have some incredible physical prowess, as well as hand-eye coordination, where they make it look like they *are* the Winchesters, they are *hunters*, they are the guys saving us from evil. You couldn't ask for more from a couple of actors. There's not a single negative thing to be said about either of those fellas. That's another fantastic thing about this show: all the way across the board everybody is into what they're doing, they're happy to be here, and everybody puts in 110 percent. This is my ninth television series, and it is definitely my favorite."

Above

The cursed rabbit's foot helped Wayne draw some lucky cards.

Opposite

Designs for key season three props: the curse boxes found in John Winchester's storage locker and Ruby's knife.

Curse Boxes

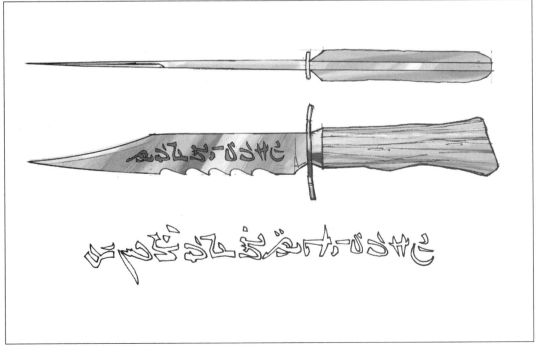

NOT SEEN ON TV: BONE KEY

Written by: Keith R.A. DeCandido

Edited by: Chris Cerasi, John Morgan, & Emily Krump

Key Characters: Sam Winchester, Dean Winchester, Bobby Singer, Alberto Fedregotti (demon), Fedra Fedregotti (demon), The Last Calusa (tribal spirit), Officer Van Montrose, President Harry S. Truman (ghost), Ernest Hemingway (ghost), Captain Terence Naylor (ghost), Caleb Dashwood (ghost of sorcerer possessing the doll Raymond), Yaphet the Poet, Nicki, Bodge, Snoopy (dog)

Opposite

The cover of *Supernatural: Bone Key*.

DID YOU KNOW?

Keith R.A. DeCandido co-edited an anthology with Josepha Sherman for Baen Books called *Urban Nightmares*, in which all the stories were based on urban legends. DeCandido's own story was about the scuba diver who's scooped up by a helicopter putting out a forest fire... and he says he's still waiting for *Supernatural* to do *that* one...

After having 'A Very Supernatural Christmas', Sam and Dean are at Bobby's house celebrating New Year's Eve when their dad's cell phone rings. It's an acquaintance of John and Dean's, Yaphet the Poet, tipping them off that the ghosts in Key West, Florida, have gone into overdrive, and people are dying... both tourists and locals alike. Bobby dismisses Yaphet as a "nut job", but the Winchester brothers hop in the Impala and drive to the sunny island.

Ghosts are not an unusual topic of conversation in Key West, which plays host to a series of ghost tours, but when one of the tour guides is found dead with his face frozen in mid-scream, the boys know they're not dealing with some publicity stunt to rope in more tourists. No one knows what horrors the guide saw, but Sam and Dean won't leave until they find out — which is fine with Dean, who's enjoying the local bar scene's live music and pretty bartenders.

Things take a turn for the weird when the brothers encounter the ghosts of the island's most famous residents, Ernest Hemingway and President Harry S. Truman. They even have several conversations with a sea captain who used to live at the guesthouse where they are staying — who died in 1871!

As they delve deeper into the mystery behind the ever-increasing and unusual spirit activity, Sam and Dean run into some nasty demons with a hidden agenda... only to discover that they're facing a mutual enemy, an ancient spirit force powerful enough — and *angry* enough — to reduce the beautiful island to a pile of bones.

FEDRA: Take *one step*, Sammy Boy, and Dean fulfills his end of the bargain half a year early.

Keith R.A. DeCandido, author of the *Supernatural* tie-in novels *Nevermore* and *Bone Key*, has had an interest in myths, folklore, and urban legends since childhood, so it's no surprise that he loves writing in the world of *Supernatural*. "I love the show and I love the characters," DeCandido enthuses.

"I also love being able to write *Supernatural* stories that embrace the location. I made an effort in both *Nevermore* and *Bone Key* to really dig into the locations of New York and Key West, and Jeff Mariotte did likewise for Arizona in *Witch's*

SUPERNATURAL
BONE KEY

AN ORIGINAL SUPERNATURAL NOVEL

Based on the hit CW series SUPERNATURAL
Keith R.A. DeCandido

Above

Novelist Keith R.A. DeCandido strikes a pose.

Canyon, because that's something that prose can do that the show can't."

Another advantage of telling a *Supernatural* story in novel form is that you can get inside characters' heads. "The camera is omniscient by nature, and a character's interior perspective is impossible to show. It's a lot of fun to get into people's heads, whether it's Dean being pissed about his father's last words to him in *Nevermore* or Sam worrying about what he's going to do if or when Dean is dead in *Bone Key*."

Delving deeper into beloved characters' personalities isn't without its pitfalls though, as the show's observant fans are likely to notice any discrepancies in the boys' portrayals. Yet DeCandido was never worried. "I find that Jared Padalecki and Jensen Ackles inhabit the characters quite well, and it was very easy to slide into their voices and personalities." Nonetheless, the novelist did hear from the fans when he got Dean's eye color wrong in *Nevermore*. "What can I say? They looked blue on my DVD player. Sigh. I not only corrected it in *Bone Key*, I joked about it at my own expense, with a woman Dean's flirting with telling him he has the most wonderful blue eyes, and Dean wondering how anyone could *possibly* think he had blue eyes." Some fans also felt Sam drove the Impala too much in *Nevermore*. "They were pretty equal with driving chores in the first season,"

BONE KEY EXCERPT

The door flew open and there were the Winchester brothers. "Hate to interrupt this meeting of Dead People Anonymous," Dean said, "but the neighbors are complaining."

"Too bad. They weren't invited," Fedra said. She let her eyes go black so the dear boys knew *exactly* what they were dealing with. "And neither are you."

It took only the slightest manipulation of power to send both young men flying across the room and crashing inelegantly into the far wall, knocking a particularly ugly painting off the wall. Fedra had been meaning to burn it in any case.

Dean tried to reach into the inner pocket of the suit he was wearing, and Fedra focused her mind on his arms, pinning them to the wall behind him. "Ah, ah, ah. No whipping out the Colt." At both brothers' surprised look, Fedra added, "Yes, we know all about your demon-killing gun. You got Azazel with it, you *won't* get us."

DeCandido points out, "but in the second they made an effort to have Dean be the only driver. Thing is, I assumed that was because of the broken arm Jared Padalecki suffered, and didn't realize it was a story decision. In any case, I made sure [in *Bone Key*] to have Dean do all the driving and have hazel eyes.

"One other complaint I got was that the horror content was pretty minimal, so I made sure to amp it up in *Bone Key*."

FEDRA: I can cast a spell that will channel all the spiritual energy on this island through a single vessel. It's a variation on what we've *been* doing. But I need a willing human vessel to do it.
DEAN: Gee, usually you just grab somebody off the street.
FEDRA: Pay attention, Dean, I said *willing*. The Last Calusa's too damn powerful — if I'm busy fighting the will of the vessel, it won't work.
DEAN: Then it won't work, 'cause I ain't *willing* to do a damn thing with your kind.
FEDRA: What, *now* you're getting all persnickety about doing a deal with a demon? Seems to me you've been down that road before when li'l bro's life was on the line. We've already established what you are, Dean — now we're just haggling over price.

DeCandido also pleased the fans by including Bobby Singer. "Bobby is an incredibly cool character, and he fit into the story nicely," says DeCandido. "I would've been perfectly happy to use either Ruby or Bela, but they *didn't* fit into the story. I would've *loved* to contrive an excuse to use Henriksen, but I couldn't make it work. I also wanted to include Ellen, but my editor cautioned me against it, since we didn't know the status of the character at the time my book took place."

The show's writers love writing the demons — what about DeCandido? "Oh, *hell* yes," he exclaims. "The demons get *all* the best lines. Not only that, I got to get into their heads, which made it even *more* fun."

Despite the important presence of demons, *Bone Key* is arguably all about the ghosts of Key West. "The only place that has more ghost stories in the US is New Orleans," DeCandido reveals. "The Naylor House is based on a real B&B on Eaton Street, and it's across the street from a building that really does have a ghost story regarding a seemingly possessed nineteenth-century doll that was a gift from a Bahamian housekeeper. Mel Fisher was also a real person, and remains a Key West legend.

"The only thing that *Bone Key* doesn't have that the show does is the physical presence of the actors," DeCandido asserts. "While that may be a huge drawback to some, I think reading *Bone Key* will show just how strong the actors and their characters are, as you'll see their personalities shine through even without Padalecki, Ackles, and Jim Beaver. The voices, the characters, the banter, the fears and hopes and dreams will all come through. Plus, it's a ripping good yarn, with more storytelling space than an episode has.

"It's a different experience from watching an episode, but still a rich one." 🖊

MUSIC

'Long Time' by Boston
'Pinball Wizard' by The Who
'House of the Rising Sun' by The Animals
'Like a Rolling Stone' by Bob Dylan
'Devil with the Blue Dress' by Mitch Ryder
'Good Golly, Miss Molly' by Little Richard
'Jenny Take a Ride' by Mitch Ryder
'Wonderful Tonight' by Eric Clapton
'Brown-Eyed Girl' by Van Morrison
'Magic Carpet Ride' by Steppenwolf
'Kashmir' by Led Zeppelin
'Tourist Town Bar' by Michael McCloud
'She Gotta Butt' by Michael McCloud
'The Conch Republic Anthem' by Michael McCloud

DO YOU BELIEVE?

HENRIKSEN: How do we survive?

Do *you* believe in the supernatural?

"Oh, my goodness, *yes* I do, and that's the problem, actually," confesses Sandra McCoy. "I fear the supernatural more than I fear real-life things that can happen, like somebody breaking into my apartment or getting into a car accident. That stuff doesn't bother me as much. If I see something out of the corner of my eye and I turn and it's not there, but I'm sure I saw somebody, that will scare me. When I bought my place in Los Angeles, Jared was very insistent that I get an alarm system and get locks on all of my doors inside, like the bedroom doors. I thought it was sweet because he was trying to be protective since he spent a lot of time in Canada. I remember him thinking that was going to make me sleep better, but it didn't because I just kept telling him that alarms and locks on the doors aren't going to protect me from ghosts! I really don't see why things like that can't exist." Even demons? "I think anything's possible, really."

Michael Massee agrees... to a certain extent. "I definitely believe there's a lot going on that we don't know about," he admits. "I believe in spirits, but I don't believe there are dead people or vampires walking around."

Sterling K. Brown isn't so quick to dismiss the notion of vampires walking among us. "Let me put it this way," he says, "I don't disbelieve. I have no reason to think they couldn't exist, but I haven't come across any. I've seen some pretty vicious hickies in my day, but nothing breaking the skin to the point that I was worried about someone."

Mercedes McNab feels that "vampire tales have been around so long that there *has to be* some truth to rumors that just won't die. I definitely had some ghosts in the old building that I lived in, but I try not to put too much thought into it or I probably will go crazy!" McNab's mental health is important to us, but so is knowing all the gory details! "There's nothing in particular to tell," McNab insists. "I just knew they were there. There was one that would always be standing right there by my door when I'd leave. I guess they were friendly ghosts, so I was lucky."

Kevin Parks considers himself lucky, too. His ghostly encounter could've taken a turn for the worse quite easily. "I lived in a house that was destined to be demolished," Parks explains. "There was an old woman's spirit in the house. My girlfriend and I encountered her three or four times. Literally, out of the corner of an eye, we'd see something walk down the hallway. We felt brushes of cold air, and my girlfriend felt a hand rub against the back of her neck once. I think the old woman knew the house was coming down and she was a little perturbed by that, since she'd raised her children there and died there and everything else. But I didn't have to

Above
True believer Harry
Spangler points out
proof that ghosts exist.

burn her bones or anything like that…"

Supernatural Magazine editor Neil Edwards has also shared his home with a ghost. "A few years ago I lived in a building that was built around the end of the nineteenth century," states Edwards. "There'd often be weird occurrences, like you'd be walking past a doorway and see a figure inside the room, then you'd look back and it'd be gone. One time, one of my flatmates and I were sitting watching TV when a picture frame on the mantelpiece literally flipped upward into the air and then fell to the ground. One of my other flatmates said he'd seen things there that he couldn't even talk about, they'd freaked him out so much. I wouldn't say I found it scary, though, just really intriguing."

Steve Boyum did not find the ghost in his house particularly scary, either. "When my daughter was a little girl she confessed that she had a ghost friend named Harvey. Things always seemed a little weird at that point; there were strange goings on in the house. Years later an actor friend of ours, Luke Askew (*Big Love*), was staying in the room upstairs from my daughter's room, and after the first night of staying there he said, 'You know, there's a ghost in this house…' He said there was a Spanish soldier that was killed by Chumash Indians on our land. I don't discount that at all, but as of late we haven't had any visits from Harvey, so either he became satisfied or he left."

Marisa Ramirez wishes that the spirit that haunted the home she grew up in would have just left. "In one of the condos there was a presence, and it would always

Above

Serious skeptic Agent Henriksen is confronted with the terrifying truth.

move the furniture around at night and the tenants would always hear things and end up moving out. We could never hold a tenant down in the place! There is definitely something out there, and it shouldn't be ignored."

Charles Malik Whitfield wouldn't dream of ignoring ghostly visitations. "My acting mentor passed away in 1999 and I was very heartbroken," Whitfield shares. "She was my best friend, and I just couldn't get it together because she was heavy on my mind and heavy in my heart. Then I remember waking up in the middle of the night and I could feel her presence. I knew she was there in the room with me. I forced myself to go back to sleep, but I heard her say, 'Get up and do what you need to do. Anything else is unacceptable.' I got up the next morning and said, 'Okay, I'm ready to go.' That was one of my most clear and vivid supernatural moments. I believe that the spirit has to move on and that we're forever connected to our ancestors and the people we love."

Paul Lougheed would add the animals we love to those beliefs. "I had one really weird experience as a teenager," Lougheed recalls. "I had a favorite cat that slept with me every night between my legs on my water bed. It was really quite annoying, to be honest, since I was afraid of rolling over and smothering it. Well, it was an old, old cat, so I had to put it down, and that night the water bed literally started doing the waves and I felt something curling up between my legs as I was falling asleep..."

"I've never had any encounters with ghosts," *Supernatural* comic book writer Rebecca Dessertine asserts, "but I've encountered angels. When I was a teenager, my grandfather was in a coma in Massachusetts, and my family raced up there from New Jersey. The entire week we were there I wouldn't go into his hospital room. I just couldn't do it. So on the sixth night, I was sitting in the waiting room and this old guy turns to me and says, 'You really should go in there, you're not going to see him for a while.' It was really weird, but not scary; it was good. So I finally went into my grandfather's room and said goodbye... and that night he died."

"I've had no weird stuff happen to me," states Kaleena Kiff, but "I can't imagine that the supernatural doesn't exist."

Richard Speight Jr. has similar beliefs. "I'm wise enough to know that I don't know everything," he contends. "So, yes, I believe there are things out there that we couldn't possibly understand or know about. I believe there are spirits and energies out there that are beyond our comprehension and probably affecting us in ways we don't realize."

Katie Cassidy senses those strange energies "sometimes when it's late at night and I'm at my place by myself. I'm like, 'What was that?' It freaks me out! Oh, my gosh, I'm a total scaredy-cat — it's so funny."

Jeremy Carver is easily freaked out as well. "Maybe there are ghosts, but I choose not to believe in the supernatural, because I would scare the crap out of myself, and I wouldn't be able to go to sleep. In fact, I used to be afraid to go into my bedroom at night, so one of my older sisters would walk into my bedroom first and check it out to make sure nothing was in there, then I could sleep. I'd go to sleep with the lights on because I always thought I saw spirits swarming around. My dad came in one night and sat on my bed for a while, then about twenty minutes after he left, the mattress, which had compressed on the bed from his weight, suddenly popped up and scared the crap out of me... and I actually never slept in that room again. So I have a healthy fear of the supernatural."

Jim Beaver chooses not to believe as well. "There are lots of things I don't understand," he remarks, "but as a general rule, I act like this is it. I don't give a lot of thought to that stuff, although it's cool to look at on TV."

A.J. Buckley has a different view on things. "There's gotta be something out there. There can't be just nothing," he insists. In fact, he recalls having a strange encounter a few years ago in the *Supernatural* wardrobe trailer... "Travis Wester was my encounter," he deadpans.

"Yeah," Wester agrees, "I think I raised the hairs on the back of A.J.'s neck.

"For my money, I think that there are always going to be limits to what human beings are able to perceive or know, and as long as those limits exist, there's going to be the supernatural, the preternatural," Wester continues. "Until human beings become omniscient — which is never going to happen — there are always going to be things outside the boundaries of our knowledge. Therefore there's always going to be something supernatural out there."

Jared Padalecki hasn't had any strange encounters on the set of *Supernatural*, "but I pay more attention," he notes. "I'm definitely aware when there's a cold draft that goes through or the lights flicker, or stuff like that. I'm always going, 'Wooo!' My beliefs haven't changed, but I'm definitely more hyperaware to the signs."

Eric Kripke's beliefs haven't change, either. "I'm still skeptical," he says, "but I want to believe in this stuff. I hope it's out there. I *want* to have an experience..." 🖉

SCARY STUFF

DEAN: We're not the ones you should be scared of...

The people who work on *Supernatural* have been known to get desensitized to the sight of ghosts and ghouls. In fact, if Jensen Ackles happens to encounter a supernatural creature, he's confident that he'll "know how to deal with it." So then, what *does* scare these brave folk?

"Growing up I was really scared of birds," Eric Kripke reveals. "I saw Hitchcock's *The Birds* and it flipped me out for life. My parents showed it to me way too young and I got scarred for life. To this day, if a bird flaps its wings right over my head, I'll jump. I'll flinch much more than a grown man should flinch at a bird flying by."

When you think of normal things that scare people, things that make your skin crawl, spiders always come to mind. "Spiders definitely scare me," Lauren Cohan agrees. "We have Black Widows in Los Angeles; I see them all the time. They scare me." Paul Lougheed feels the same way. "Going back to my childhood, I got a bite from a spider called the Hobbit Spider. They're monsters *and* they're poisonous. For most people, it's just an allergic reaction — I think they kill maybe one person every fifty years — but the bite really swells up."

Laurence Andries doesn't want to admit he's afraid of spiders. "I know my friends," he explains, "and when they read this, they're going to use this against me. I have a deathly fear of spiders. If I were to go in a room with twenty thousand of them, like on *Fear Factor*, that'd be it, I'd be done — I'd just shut down."

The other thing that people tend to be afraid of is public speaking. "Getting up in front of people is pretty scary," Phil Sgriccia admits. "That's why I don't do it. That's why I'm on the side of the camera that I'm on!" Mercedes McNab has a similar fear. "Singing in public scares me, actually," she confesses. "I hyperventilate. I just can't do it."

"I'm not afraid of public speaking," Sera Gamble asserts, "but I know myself as a public speaker, and I know that when I'm in a high-pressure situation like that, something dumb will come out of my mouth. I accept that I'm gonna have a flub, so I move forward under the assumption that I'll make a fool of myself, at least a little bit. I'm one of those people who are scared of the creepy crawly things. My rule of thumb is if it moves really fast with no legs, then it's scary — snakes terrify me — and if it has a really unnecessary number of legs, then it scares me. I don't understand centipedes and millipedes — they completely freak me out. Ben Edlund was in my office one day and we were looking at You Tube videos — I mean, we were working really, really hard — and he clicked on a link to a giant centipede killing a mouse! I was so traumatized that I had to leave the room. And he continues to threaten that he's going to force me to watch it because he knows that

I'm too scared of it. Scorpions and spiders and the slithery things, I can do without them. I'm a city girl."

Kim Manners would gladly do without the slithery things, too. "Snakes scare me," he states. "When I was a little kid, my dad was doing a series called *Naked City* in New York. We lived just under the Lincoln Tunnel in New Jersey, and we had a creek running through our backyard. One day there was a water moccasin in it, and the neighbour had pulled it out and cut its head off. I ran to see what was going on and as I was running, the head (that was already cut off from the snake) jumped up and grabbed my jeans cuff and tried to bite me. So I don't like snakes... And I don't like lizards. I hate reptiles. Nothing else scares me. Although, I don't like bears."

Lou Bollo believes you'd have to be crazy not to be afraid of bears. "I've spent a lot of time up north and in the mountains, up in Grizzly country, and I've had a number of encounters with Grizzly bears. That's the most scared I've ever been, and I have nightmares over it. It's this actual 700-pound thing that in a split second can just tear you wide open. I've been treed by them. I've had them come by my tent on salmon rivers, bump the tent with their noses. I've had them show up in the opening of a cook tent and look inside at us when we have no firearms because we left them outside. And you think, 'Well, I guess that's it.'"

Bears are truly terrifying, but they're not the only fearsome furred animals in the woods. "The absolute truth of what freaks me out more than anything is raccoons," states Sterling K. Brown. "They're nocturnal creatures, they're sewer dwellers, and

Above
Jensen Ackles and
Jared Padalecki are
confident when facing
supernatural horrors
with guns and knives,
but that won't help
them against
earthquakes.

when you're coming home late at night you see a family of 'coons crawling out of the sewer together. The thing about raccoons, unlike any other sort of furry woodland creature, is that they don't clear a path when people come. A squirrel will scamper out of your way, a rabbit will just bounce away, but raccoons look at you like, 'How dare you invade *my* territory.'"

Jared Padalecki's big dogs get freaked out by raccoons, too. "I have a deck outside of my master bedroom, so the dogs will sleep on their dog beds by the window, and I'll be in bed sleeping, and all of a sudden, in the middle of the night, Sadie will bark her head off, and I jump awake, thinking, 'What's going on? What's going on?' My heart's beating so fast and I *know* it's just the dog barking at a raccoon, but I can't get back to sleep. I guess it's that weird kind of unknown thing."

A.J. Buckley can relate to being home alone at night. "Here's what really scares me," he says. "At three o'clock in the morning, you wake up, you gotta take a whiz, and you go into the bathroom, and it's really dark and you can just kind of make yourself out when you look in the mirror. That scares me because I'm always afraid I'm going to look in the mirror and see some dude standing behind me with a hook for a hand and he'll just slice me from my groin to my gullet..."

Chris Lennertz has a similar fear of a 'hook man' or worse stalking him in the mists late at night. "My office is down by Marina Del Rey. A lot of times I'll work until three o'clock in the morning and then drive home. Being by the ocean, you get that insane fog. There have been times where I finish up a cue on *Supernatural* and then I walk out the door and I can't see more than two or three feet in front of my face into the mist. There definitely are times where I'll open the door really fast, look both ways, then run to my car, get right in it and quickly lock the door. There's definitely a little paranoia involved."

Nonetheless, Lennertz says, "The thing that scares me the most is the idea of being trapped, in terms of asphyxiation. I definitely have a fear of running out of air. The idea of being buried alive is the creepiest..."

"Buried alive!" Charles Beeson exclaims. "Let's put that down as my big fear."

Robert Singer also has a great fear of being trapped. "I get more claustrophobic with age," he admits. "If I'm in a really claustrophobic situation I get quite scared. There's an episode that Kim directed in year two where the ghost was in the wall ['No Exit'] and I got claustrophobic just watching it. The actors were definitely boxed in. It was shot on one of those itty-bitty cameras that you can snake in, so it was tight quarters. Just watching it I get the willies."

Keith R.A. DeCandido can appreciate the fear of being trapped. "My biggest fear is being physically restrained," he says. "If I'm ever arrested and handcuffed, I'll probably freak."

What freaks Jared Padalecki out is earthquakes. "I grew up in Texas," he points out. "We have thunderstorms and lightning and stuff like that, and that was always kind of cool, because you could watch from inside, where you're not getting wet, and every now and then the power would go out. But the first time I was in Los Angeles and an earthquake happened, it rocked my world — literally. I was like, 'This is the ground I'm standing on. Why is it moving, why is that building shaking?' It changes the way you think about everything. You can't even trust the ground you're walking on!

"Earthquakes are scary," Padalecki emphasizes, "and I'm not a chicken or anything. Some people I know aren't scared of earthquakes at all. For them, it's kind of fun. One of my best friends, Jordan, will not go into the ocean, because he's like, 'Dude, *sharks*!' And I'm like, 'What are you talking about?' I'll scuba dive, I'll snorkel, I'll do anything. 'Oh, they're not going to get you — they could, but it's not going to happen.' I'm not scared of sharks, but he's not scared of earthquakes…"

Chances are Jerry Wanek's afraid of sharks, too, since he says, "I've got a pretty healthy fear of a lot of things… I don't like darkness and I don't like loneliness. I'd rather be in a group of people. I have a very wild imagination, so some of the scariest places I can be are simply exist inside my head. I can't spend too much time alone, because I watched too many horror shows growing up and I'm afraid of what's going to come out of the graveyards.

"I'm afraid of *what's around the corner…*" ✍

Below

Sam and Dean have no fear of the supernatural, but they're not so keen on clowns and flying.

SUPERNATURAL REACTION

"Supernatural is first-rate horror story-telling. Stylish and atmospheric, it is rooted in complex performances by its leads, the private pain and rage their characters feel leading them elegantly into mysteries which have some genuinely powerful terrors at their heart. To lose *Supernatural* would be, in short, a crying shame." — Clive Barker, March 2007

In its third year, rather than showing the creative fatigue that sometimes affects long-running shows, "*Supernatural* is on top of its game!" declared Matt Rousch of *TV Guide*. It's not likely a single viewer would argue with that. In fact, the fans are making their opinions known, such as Gloria Atwater of VampiresAndSlayers.net, who says, "If you want television that scares, tantalizes, enthralls and engages, not to mention surprisingly touches your heart, you want *Supernatural*. The acting is brilliant, the writing witty and thoughtful, and there is a strong internal story-arc that holds the show together."

"The fans of this show are so intense," notes Sterling K. Brown. "They love the show so much that it makes me feel that much better to be a part of it. It's nice to be a part of something that people are so passionate about." Brown encountered fans first-hand at the 2008 Asylum convention, which originally had Jared Padalecki on the guest list, though the star had to bow out due to scheduling conflicts with filming of the latest *Friday the 13th* feature film. Jensen Ackles was also unable to attend, but he mentions that they're "getting more and more offers for these conventions, and Jared and I are trying to make more of an attempt to meet the fans and shake hands and stuff like that. Our whole production is making efforts to get us out to do those things, because it's such an amazing support system. It's cool, and I'm glad that those opportunities are arising."

Of course, the stars of the show have a lot to do with the level of fan response. As Karla Peterson of SignOnSanDiego.com puts it, "Much of this spooky show's appeal comes from the earthly charms of Ackles and Padalecki, whose combative chemistry has the harsh ring of brotherly truth." Atwater echoes her sentiments: "The chemistry between these two talented actors is electric, and they deliver the entire spectrum, from sarcasm to angst to kickass action with complete believability." Or as Connie Ogle of *The Miami Herald* puts it, "You can keep your McDreamys and McSteamys. The hottest guys on TV can be found on The CW, driving the back roads in a black '67 Impala..."

Ogle goes on to say, "Sam and Dean aren't the only great-looking elements, though.

Supernatural's camerawork is excellent, and its transfer to DVD is sharp." The season three DVD box-set also features short segments showcasing favorite aspects of seven episodes (by Kim Manners, Eric Kripke, Ben Edlund, Ivan Hayden, and Sera Gamble), a gag reel, and featurettes on the show's effects, the Impala, and the Ghostfacers. In a cool promotion, some of the DVD sets available for purchase at Best Buy in North America even contain a collectible 1:64-scale 1967 Chevrolet Impala die-cast car that closely replicates the Impala driven across the country by the Winchesters.

Back for the third season is Inkworks' *Supernatural* trading cards, and this set was preceded by a special 'Connections' set, too. As Inkworks president Allan Caplan explains it, the Connections sets "focus on the relationships between characters and how those relationships change over time. The relationships in *Supernatural* are key to understanding and appreciating the series, so it was a perfect fit for our Connections format. Fans and collectors of our *Supernatural:* Season One and Season Two trading cards indicated to us that they wanted more than just annual season-based sets. We felt like the demand was strong and the time was right for a *Supernatural:* Connections set."

Demand has also been strong for the *Supernatural* comic tie-in line, which features John Winchester as a young hunter with his sons in tow. Entitled 'Rising Son', the second mini-series once again is written by co-executive producer Peter Johnson, this time joined by co-writer Rebecca Dessertine, who just so happens to be creator Eric Kripke's assistant. "That was a stroke of luck," Dessertine admits. "We were having a going-away party for the girl who'd had my position, and Eric's

Above

Cover of issue one of the second *Supernatural* tie-in comic mini-series, *Rising Son*.

standing around and he just sort of blithely says, 'So, if anyone wants to write the comic book with Peter...' My heart raced!" Needless to say, she contacted Johnson right away.

"It's an improvement over the first arc," Kripke feels. "They've done a better job of capturing what I think is unique about the prequel story arc, which is this bizarre family dynamic of a father trying to raise his two boys and killing monsters at the same time. Peter and Rebecca have done a much better job focusing on that." With that storyline came the early hints of Sam's special connection to the supernatural realm. "What we tried to do is explain why John would even think perhaps there's something going on with Sam," Dessertine reveals. "We're filling in that blank."

Diego Olmos took over illustrating the comic series, and Kripke couldn't be happier. "The new art is a big improvement. The problem with the first series was the art was too stylized and it wasn't gory enough. I kept saying to Peter, 'You get to show things we're not allowed to show on the TV show. Why the hell aren't we showing all the gore that we can't show on network television?' I think the new artist did an incredible job — the art is beautiful, scary and gory."

Perhaps Kripke's favorite piece of *Supernatural* merchandise is the collector's plate. "I think it's so funny that we have a decorative plate. On the back of it, it says, 'Warning, do not use this plate for food. It is dangerous to eat off this plate.' So it's a plate that you're not allowed to use as a plate. I love it!"

Jared Padalecki is still not used to seeing his face on plates or T-shirts, or even DVD box-sets. "It always weirds me out," he admits, "but otherwise it's kind of flattering."

"The replica pieces sell best for *Supernatural*," says Marianne Ward of Power Star Collectibles. "Dean's ring and Sam's bracelet — anything that has been featured on the show. We've also done well with the calendars and items featuring the car."

"The busts are fun, too," Kripke points out. "I think they're really cool sculptures." Mark Del Vecchio, president of CineQuest.com, makers of the minibusts, couldn't agree more. When asked what prompted the decision to make *Supernatural* minibusts, he responds, "First and foremost, it's a great show! We love it! Who can resist a complex mythology, wonderful characters and scary

Below

Cover of *Rising Son* issue two.

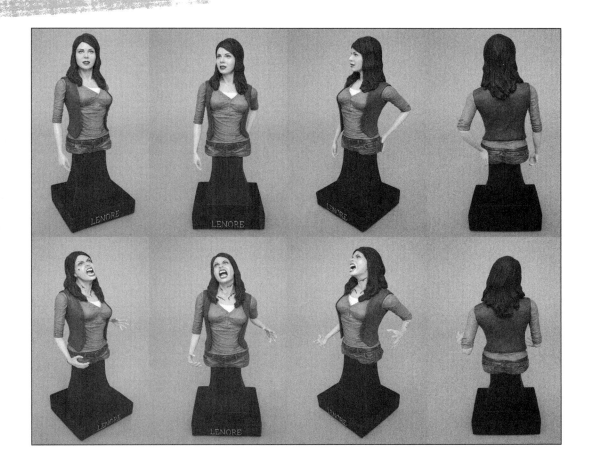

monsters? Second, the response to *Supernatural* in our retail store has been very strong; sales were a good indicator that the fans would fiercely support the show and would buy *Supernatural* collectibles."

While fans would no doubt love to be able to buy busts of all their favorite characters and monsters, that wouldn't be feasible "because of the time it takes to create the minibusts (sketches first, then prototyping, sculpting, painting, production, and shipping). At the time we began the process, we were drawing mostly from the first season. And with our approach — trying to capture not only the character but key moments in their episode, rather than producing static character busts — we took some time to pick key moments for key characters. We wanted to do Dean Winchester in 'Wendigo' first as we loved Jensen Ackles' performance and intensity in the scene from that episode. John Winchester from 'Devil's Trap' was irresistible. Of the monsters, the first season was difficult, as the audience didn't get a close look at many of them. The scarecrow was a 'no brainer' — *Wizard of Oz* pun intended — because the look they created was so intense; same with the Hook Man. Plus, we loved the urban legend backdrop to that character, as well as the opportunity to capture the hook and chain."

Above
CineQuest's bust of vampire Lenore from 'Bloodlust', as portrayed by Amber Benson.

The third wave of minibusts features the vampire Lenore, as portrayed by Amber Benson. "The Lenore character gave us a chance to do a couple of things," Del Vecchio explains. "First, to create a human and a vampire version of a minibust. And second, to give fans of both *Buffy the Vampire Slayer* and *Supernatural* a version of Amber Benson as a vampire."

As cool as the Lenore and John Winchester minibusts are, the big question on fans' minds is, 'When will we see a Sam minibust?' "We are still working on the Sam sculpt, trying to get him just right. He will be produced in early 2009," Del Vecchio states. "Interest in the minibusts continues to grow. We've had wonderful emails from those who own the busts."

Kripke believes that "Sam and Dean and all of our monsters would make a great action figure line." In fact, CineQuest.com is rumored to have twelve-inch *Supernatural* action figures in the works. "Yes," Del Vecchio confirms, "we are still working on the sculpts for those, as well as the clothing. We expect to announce something in early 2009 when we've got a schedule locked down and some great prototypes to show."

And Del Vecchio adds tantalizingly, "We have some other *Supernatural* items in the works that are pending approval from Warner Bros. As soon as we can, we'll make an announcement that I know will please fans."

CineQuest.com doesn't just sell the minibusts, so what other *Supernatural* merchandise has been the most popular? "That's a tough one to answer," states Del Vecchio. "Sales across the board have been very strong; we haven't seen a show like this sales-wise since *Buffy*! T-shirts and posters have sold well, as have mugs. I'd say the Inkworks trading cards and the replica 'Mask' amulet that Dean wears, made by Creation, have been among the most popular. Sales of the two comic book series as well as Titan's official *Supernatural Magazine* have far surpassed projections and even our wildest expectations."

"I love the magazine," Kripke concurs. "It's well put together. I'm really impressed by it."

"The reaction [to the magazine] has been amazing," says magazine editor Neil Edwards. "*Supernatural* attracts a hugely devoted and knowledgeable fan base, one that isn't afraid to speak up. I'm pleased to say that the readers really engage with the magazine just like they do for the show, and I love that." And Edwards would know — he was a part of that fan base long before he started editing the magazine.

"I'd always been a fan of shows like *The X-Files*, *Buffy the Vampire Slayer*, and *Angel*, and when they finished, it seemed like there wouldn't be anything on TV that could take their place. Then, when I happened across *Supernatural*, I immediately got into it, what with the scares, the comedy, the great writing, and the central relationship between Sam and Dean. I have an older brother too, so I can definitely relate to Sam! I spent my formative years at rock or metal clubs and concerts, so the soundtrack rang quite a few bells with me as well. When the magazine started I was editing another magazine but contributing to some of the features in *Supernatural Magazine* as well, so I was thrilled to take over the editorship from Kate Lloyd when she was promoted.

"It's amazing editing a magazine that's all about a show I'm a huge fan of," Edwards enthuses. "I get to immerse myself in the show every day, find out more about the making of it, decide which elements of the show to produce features on, and perhaps most excitingly, find out secrets about the show before most of the other fans!

"We're very lucky to have access to all the people behind the show, people like Eric Kripke, Jared Padalecki, and Jensen Ackles, as well as the producers, the writers, the directors, the crew — everyone who makes the show what it is — and they share their secrets, stories, news, and views with us. Like the show itself, we're also

immersed in the mythology of the supernatural and explore some of those subjects, so it's a great place to pursue that interest. If you love Sam and Dean (and if you're reading this, I'm sure you do...), there are also tons of posters and other pictures of them to enjoy!

"If you're a fan of the show, it's *the* place to go (along with the companion guides, of course!) to find out more about everything that goes into the making of it. Sometimes when you love a show, you'll see coverage of it in general entertainment magazines or on websites written by people who often don't like the show or don't even seem to know much about it," Edwards adds. "That isn't the case with *Supernatural Magazine* — we love the show just as much as the readers do, and I think that really comes across when you read it."

That's just it; everyone who's watched *Supernatural* loves the show. So if you know anyone who's been living under a rock (black or otherwise) that hasn't seen *Supernatural* yet, tell them what Karl Cramer of *Wizard* told his readers: "You can jump into any episode and have a great time." Better yet, pass along Gloria Atwater's message: "*Supernatural* is just too good to miss." *

16 Things To Do Before I Die

By Dean Winchester

1. Eat cheeseburgers. Lots and lots of cheeseburgers. ✓
2. Visit 'Gumby Girl'. ✓
3. Catalogue the contents of dad's storage locker. ✗
4. Memorize some exorcisms. (Well, at least one...) ✗
5. Investigate the legend behind the fairy tale Jack and the Beanstalk. (Can hellhounds climb giant beanstalks?) ✗
6. Find another Hand of Glory. If those suckers really can open any locked doors, having one could come in <u>handy</u> in our line of work. ✗
7. Kill Gordon. ✓
8. Try a piece of Christmas fruitcake. (How bad could it be?) ✗
9. See if Bobby has any amulets that protect against hex bag mojo. ✓

10. ~~Dreamwalk in Lisa's head to see if she's having any naughty dreams about me... and find out if she was telling the truth about Ben.~~ (That kid was freakin' <u>Mini-Me</u> — he's gotta have some Dean DNA!) ✗

11. Find a real mystery spot — could use it as a last ditch escape route when the hellhounds come calling. ✗

12. Kill Lilith. ✗

13. Figure out a way to get that damn Ghostfacers theme song out of my head. ✓

14. Try to call dad for real on Edison's Spirit Phone. (If it doesn't work, order some pizza.) ✗

15. Get the Colt back and use it to show Doc Benton exactly what I understand about "immortality"... ✗

16. Don't go to Hell.

TITAN BOOKS

TAKE A SPOOKY ROAD TRIP THROUGH THE DARK HEART OF AMERICA...

OUT NOW!

SUPERNATURAL
THE OFFICIAL COMPANION
SEASON 1

NICHOLAS KN

SUPERNATURAL
THE OFFICIAL COMPANION
SEASON 2

NICHOLAS KNIGHT